# EDWARD I

Edward I

# 𝕰𝖉𝖜𝖆𝖗𝖉 I

## L. F. SALZMAN

D.Litt., C.B.E.

"Thah mi tonge were mad of stel
Ant mi harte y-yote of bras,
The goodnesse myht I never telle
That with Kyng Edward was.
Kyng as thou art cleped conqueror,
In uch bataille thou hadest pris.
God bringe thi soule to the honour
That ever wes aut ever ys,
That lesteth ay withouten ende!
Bidde we God ant oure Lady
To thilke blisse Jesus us sende."

## FREDERICK A. PRAEGER

*Publishers*

NEW YORK · WASHINGTON

BOOKS THAT MATTER

Published in the United States of America in 1968
by Frederick A. Praeger, Inc., Publishers
111 Fourth Avenue, New York, N.Y. 10003

Library of Congress Catalog Card Number: 68-25473
Printed in Great Britain

To
PROFESSOR VIVIAN GALBRAITH
I dedicate this book,
which owes its existence
largely to his kind
encouragement

# Contents

# Illustrations

*For the photographs of the carvings of Edward, Eleanor and Margaret we are indebted to the kindness of Mr. John Harvey.*

# Preface

Historians of the nineteenth century tended to overstress the influence of personalities on the course of history. Modern historians, following the anti-hero pose of recent literature, are more apt to minimise this influence and assert that no individual has seriously affected the development of civilisation which we call history. Personally I find it difficult to write off Mahomet, Napoleon and even Hitler as negligible phenomena, or even to regard the individuality of many less outstanding figures as entirely ephemeral. Anyhow, in this study of one of our greatest Kings I have tried to bring out his personality. My account is based upon contemporary chronicles and record material, indicated in the list of Sources, and the conclusions drawn are my own.

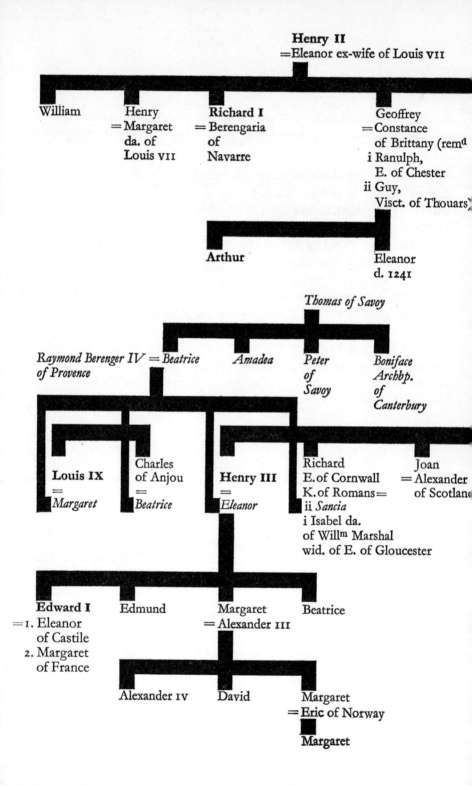

**Henry II**
=Eleanor ex-wife of Louis VII

William

Henry
=Margaret
da. of
Louis VII

**Richard I**
=Berengaria
of
Navarre

Geoffrey
=Constance
of Brittany (rem^d
i Ranulph,
E. of Chester
ii Guy,
Visct. of Thouars)

**Arthur**

Eleanor
d. 1241

*Thomas of Savoy*

*Raymond Berenger IV = Beatrice
of Provence*

*Amadea*

*Peter
of
Savoy*

*Boniface
Archbp.
of
Canterbury*

**Louis IX**
=
*Margaret*

Charles
of Anjou
=
*Beatrice*

**Henry III**
=
*Eleanor*

Richard
E. of Cornwall
K. of Romans =
ii *Sancia*
i Isabel da.
of Will^m Marshal
wid. of E. of Gloucester

Joan
= Alexander
of Scotland

**Edward I**
=1. Eleanor
of Castile
2. Margaret
of France

Edmund

Margaret
= Alexander III

Beatrice

Alexander IV

David

Margaret
= Eric of Norway

Margaret

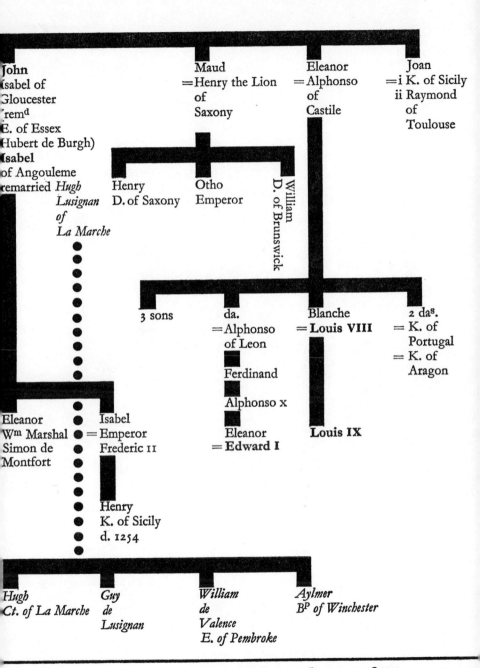

# The Descendants of Henry II

# Chapter One

# The Lord Edward

The workings of the mysterious influence of heredity present few greater puzzles than the characters of the English kings. It is indeed strange that Edward I should have been the son of the pious but incapable Henry III and father of the equally incapable Edward II. To support any theory of inherited characteristics we must pass beyond his grandfather, the infamous John, to Henry II, in whose vigorous individuality were prominent many of those features of character which can be traced in his descendant. By a curious coincidence both Henry and Edward reigned for thirty-five years, and by a coincidence less curious and more explicable each engaged in struggles with the power of the Baronage and of the Church, and each won for himself a place among the great law-givers of the nation. Other resemblances, more or less close, might be traced between these two great kings, but there was one great difference in their histories; Henry II fought his way to the throne and gained the kingship by force of arms, Edward I was the recognised heir to the crown from the day of his birth and succeeded unchallenged.

Henry III was in his thirtieth year when, in 1236, he married Eleanor, daughter of Raymond of Provence and sister of Queen Margaret of France, and it was not until more than three years later that any child was born of this marriage. On the night of 17 June 1239, Eleanor gave birth to a son. In spite of the unpopularity of the queen the citizens of London gave the infant an enthusiastic welcome; the houses were illuminated and the streets thronged with processions, singing, shouting, and thumping drums. The nobles were not behindhand with their congratulations, and Henry saw to it that those to whom he sent the glad tidings showed themselves duly appreciative of the compliment and expressed their pleasure in a substantial manner. He had himself bestowed lands worth £10 a year upon Robert de Stopham, who had brought him the good news; and when his messengers returned he enquired very thoroughly into the nature and value of the gifts sent in reply and if any, though valuable, did not come up to his expectation he sent them back with an intimation that more was required. So greedily did the royal father act in his extortion of presents that it was said at court—"God gave us this child but the king is selling it to us". On the fourth day after his birth the boy was baptised with much ceremony at Westminster. The Bishop of Carlisle performed the first part of the ceremony but the actual baptism was administered by the legate Otho, although he was only in deacon's orders and the Archbishop of Canterbury was present. By the king's special wish he was named after Edward the Confessor, to whose memory Henry professed great devotion and on whose weakest traits he moulded his own character with unfortunate success. Among Edward's sponsors were his uncles Richard, Earl of Cornwall, and Simon de Montfort, Earl of Leicester, Humphrey de Bohun, Earl of Essex, Piers de Mauley and Amauri de St. Amand; and of the crowd of nobles and ladies present a large proportion were, like Montfort, Mauley and St. Amand, foreign courtiers. Two children of humble rank, Philip son of Richard the tailor and Peter son of Emma, having the good fortune to be baptised later in the day in the same font as the young prince, benefited by the grant of small yearly pensions. Shortly afterwards little Edward was established at Windsor, under the care of Hugh Giffard, whose wife Sybil had acted as midwife to Queen Eleanor. Having thus arranged for his temporal welfare his pious parents saw to it that his spiritual welfare was not neglected. A tunic of fine samite, made to the measure of the royal infant, was sent to the church of St. Mary at Southwark, to be placed upon the crucifix there; a chantry was established for him at Windsor, furnished with all needful vestments and ornaments and served by a resident chaplain; and at Christmas fifteen poor men were given a good meal, a tunic, a pair of shoes, and a penny on his behalf.

For some years there is naturally little to record beyond payments to the child's nurses, Alice and Sarah, and other attendants, gifts, such as a ring bought from Mathew of Venice and given to him with his father's blessing on New Year's Day, 1244, or purchases of necessaries for his household. Some of the articles bought for his diet would hardly be considered suitable at the present day. The wisdom of giving wine to a child in his third year might be doubted; but it was certainly wise of King Henry to send two casks of "good and delicate wine" when he learnt that the wine was unwholesome which had been provided for little Edward and the other children at Windsor—among whom was Henry of Almaine, Edward's cousin and senior by a few months. It is possibly not a mere coincidence that an order was given for lampreys to be supplied regularly for Edward's use in 1242 and that in September of that year he fell ill; his father at once sent round to all the religious houses near London, desiring their prayers, and the child recovered. Four years later, in 1246, on his seventh birthday, Edward was down in Hampshire with his parents at the dedication of the abbey church of Beaulieu and was there again taken ill. His mother insisted upon staying with him in the abbey and remained there nearly three weeks; this was an infringement of the monastic rule against allowing women to lodge within their precincts, and for permitting it the prior and cellarer were afterwards deposed.

Soon after Edward had reached the responsible age of

twelve he began to take part in public affairs. As early as 1243 Henry had been persuaded by Eleanor to bestow the revenues of Gascony upon their son; these revenues were at the time in the hands of Richard, Earl of Cornwall, and the attempt to make him surrender them led to a violent quarrel, but in the end the king forced them from him. A series of Seneschals were appointed, under whom things in Gascony went from bad to worse until in 1248 Simon de Montfort was appointed Lieutenant for six years. Simon's vigorous government restored some kind of order temporarily but soon united all sections of the province against himself, until in 1252 Henry found himself obliged to cancel Simon's appointment, reiterate the grant to Edward, and promise that next year either he himself or Edward would come over to Gascony. Early in 1253 the new King of Castile, Alphonso X, encouraged by the anarchy prevailing in Gascony, laid claim to the province, and Henry was obliged to defend his possessions. Accordingly, on 6 August, he took a tender and tearful farewell of his son and sailed from Portsmouth, Edward standing on the shore weeping and sobbing, and refusing to leave as long as he could see the bellying sails of the ships. Henry's troops gained several successes and he brought the campaign to a close by a stroke of diplomacy which proved happier in its eventual results than might have been expected. John Mansel, Provost of Beverly, greatest of pluralists and most trusted of royal clerks, was charged with a mission to Alphonso to obtain peace and an alliance by the betrothal of Edward to Alphonso's sister Eleanor. The terms were gladly accepted; Alphonso renounced his claims to Gascony, offered certain concessions to the English pilgrims visiting the popular shrine of St. James of Compostella, and agreed to the marriage of his sister to young Edward, only stipulating that the prince should be sent to him that he might see that he was worthy in mind and body. Henry in return promised to endow

Eleanor richly and to allow Edward, to whom he had just granted Ireland, 15,000 marks a year. Edward's sister Beatrice, born in 1242, was also to be sent with him to be married to one of the Spanish king's brothers, and Henry undertook to join Alphonso in a crusade against the Moors and to help him against other enemies, especially the King of Navarre. Orders were therefore sent for Queen Eleanor to cross with her children and join Henry at Bordeaux; but their start was delayed by an outbreak of the ancient quarrel between the rival fleets of Yarmouth and the Cinque Ports. Probably with the idea of avoiding jealousy between these fierce rivals, it had been arranged that Prince Edward should cross in a ship of Yarmouth and Queen Eleanor and her suite in ships from Winchelsea. Unfortunately the ship from Yarmouth was much larger and better fitted than those of the Portsmen—a fact that was no doubt tactlessly emphasised by its crew; the Winchelsea men promptly stormed the offending vessel and carried off its great mast, which they installed on the queen's ship. The queen was naturally much frightened, and when the news reached Henry he sent orders that she was not to cross. By this time, however, the affair had settled down, and when her husband's message reached her she exclaimed:—"Troubles arise on every side! All things are prepared for the journey, I have said goodbye to everybody, the wind is blowing in the right direction, and shall I turn back? Far be it from me!" So on 6 June she sailed from Portsmouth with her two sons, Edward and Edmund, forty knights and her household, under the charge of her uncle, Boniface, Archbishop of Canterbury, and on 12 June they reached Bordeaux. In October Edward crossed the border into Castile and was met by Alphonso, who bestowed the honour of knighthood upon him, in preparation for his marriage at Burgos. Towards the end of the year Edward returned to Bordeaux, where he was received "like an angel of God" by his father.

B

Eleanor of Castile was destined in after years to win the affection of her husband's subjects, but at the time the match was unpopular. Spaniards were disliked and rather despised, and it was felt that Alphonso was too far off and too much surrounded by his own enemies to be of much value as an ally against France. The feeling against the Spaniards was intensified by the pride, luxury and greed of the embassy brought over in 1255 by Sanchez, Bishop-elect of Toledo and brother of King Alphonso, to treat for the marriage of the Princess Beatrice. When at last Eleanor herself landed at Dover, Edward being still in Gascony, she brought with her so many of her compatriots that it seemed as if the Spaniards intended to seize the country. The Londoners, always ready for pageantry and display, welcomed her with pealing bells, songs and processions. Her lodging had been adorned by the splendour-loving King Henry with silken hangings and rugs, and even with carpets—one of those Spanish refinements of luxury which made the citizens gape and scoff. The Spaniards were amazed and delighted with the honour shown them, but the more serious citizens, seeing in these foreigners merely successors to the hordes of Poitevins and Savoyards already battening on the land, wondered grimly why the English alone should be the race despised and neglected by their own king. It may therefore be doubted what weight there was behind the pomp and applause with which Edward was welcomed to London on his return at the end of November. An incident, however, which occurred in the following year, 1256, showed his character in a favourable light, and his popularity must have been increased by his falling out of favour with his father. The merchants of Gascony came to the young prince and complained of the robbery and extortion which they suffered at the hands of the royal purveyors and other officials, who took their goods and made no payments, a thing which even the very Saracens were too honest to do. Edward, finding that their complaints were justified, went to his father and reproached him angrily, saying that he would not allow such injustice to continue in his lands. Henry at first adopted an air of aggrieved innocence, comparing himself to Henry II when his beloved sons rebelled against him, but at last gave in and agreed to remedy the evil. Men considered it as something more than a coincidence that at the time of this quarrel with his father Edward increased his household and began to ride about with two hundred horse in his train; but this may well have been due to his recognition of his own growing importance as a prince and a knight. It was in June of this year that he attended his first tournament, at Blythe, and was initiated into the laws and regulations of those chivalric contests of which he afterwards became so great a devotee.

Unfortunately the tact and wise consideration for their welfare displayed by Edward towards his Gascon subjects was not exhibited towards the Welsh, though we may perhaps regard the disastrous policy adopted towards them as emanating less from Edward himself than from Sir Geoffrey de Langley, his deputy. The portions of Wales made over to the prince were a district in the north centred on Rhuddlan, and Montgomery, Carmarthen and Cardigan in the south. The attempt to introduce English laws, coupled with the oppression and extortions of Sir Geoffrey and his subordinates, culminating in a poll-tax of fifteen pence, drove the Welsh into rebellion in the autumn of 1256. They found a leader in the warlike prince Llewelyn ap Gruffudd, who had just defeated and expelled his Anglophile brothers Owain and David. With Llewelyn was joined Maredudd, son of Rhys the Hoarse, and under these two chieftains the lands of Edward and of his chief native supporter, Gruffudd ap Gwenwynwyn of Bromfield, were laid waste. Edward appealed first for aid to his father; but Henry had no money to spare and had already repented of the generosity with which he had

enriched his son to his own impoverishment; he therefore told him bluntly that the lands had been given to
him and he must look after them himself. A visit to his
wealthy uncle Richard of Cornwall at Wallingford produced a loan of 4,000 marks, but the money proved of
little use, as the winter storms rendered the marshy
valleys and wind-swept mountains inaccessible, and the
Welsh ravaged with impunity up to Chester. The Welsh
mocked openly at Edward's impotence, and when he
threatened to bring over the Irish and smash them like
a potter's vessel, they retorted by fitting out armed
galleys to intercept the Irish transports. North and South
Wales were for once united, and about Midsummer, 1257,
an English force under Sir Stephen Bausan and Sir
Robert Norreys was annihilated on the borders of
Carmarthen. This compelled Henry to take the field, and
he assembled an army at Chester in August. When the
weather became inclement, early in October, the king
and his courtiers retired to the comfort of Westminster
and left the Welsh to continue their ravaging unchecked.

The Welsh muddle did not tend to increase Edward's
popularity. English sympathy was largely on the side of
the Welsh, who, it was felt, had justice on their side and
were setting their neighbours a good example in defend-
ing their rights against the aggression of foreigners.
Moreover the troops which Edward had collected were
ruffianly foreign mercenaries, and the members of his
household were little better. In all the towns and villages
where they were quartered they bullied and plundered
the inhabitants, and at the very time that their master was
borrowing money from Earl Richard in Wallingford
Castle they broke into Wallingford Priory, demanding
food, seized what they wanted, broke up the furniture,
and maltreated the monks and their servants. The prince
himself was liable to those outbursts of passion which
characterised his family; on one occasion when hawking
along the river bank he lost his temper with his com-

panion on the other side of the stream and abused him
roundly for mismanaging the hawk. His companion
retorting to his threats that it was just as well that the
stream divided them, he turned his horse's head, plunged
in, and gaining the other bank pursued the offender
with drawn sword, only sparing him when he discreetly
offered no resistance. On another occasion Edward ordered
the savage mutilation of an unfortunate youth who had
got in his way. Nor was the alacrity with which he mort-
gaged his lands to William de Valence for a supply of
ready money regarded as a favourable omen for the
future. Events, however, were now maturing that were
destined to exercise a sobering effect upon the young
prince and to bring out the best features of his character.
The insolence of the king's foreign favourites, and
especially of his Poitevin half-brothers, had at last
exasperated the greater nobles into action and they had
found a leader in Simon de Montfort, Earl of Leicester,
brother-in-law of King Henry. At a parliament held in
Oxford in June 1258, the national party succeeded in
forcing the appointment of a committee, including the
Earls of Leicester, Gloucester, Hereford, and Norfolk,
to draw up certain anti-foreign measures and to reform
various abuses of legal and feudal customs. To their
"provisions" the king and his son were required to
swear consent. Henry, for whom oaths had little value,
gave his oath without hesitation but Edward, who
always preferred to avoid breaking a pledge when possible,
was only induced to give his assent with great reluctance.
Their difference of opinion as to the value of an oath
appears to have led to a slight quarrel between the father
and son, but they were reconciled on meeting at Winchester a little later and together attended the consecration of the new cathedral church at Salisbury at the end
of September.

Early in the following year, 1259, Edward was appealed to on behalf of the squirehood, or lesser gentry,

of England, who complained that the Barons, having got their own way at Oxford, had failed to carry out their promises of reforms. He replied that he had taken the oath reluctantly but that having taken it he would stand to it and would die, if needs be, for the good of the commonwealth, and, acting up to the spirit of his words, he brought pressure to bear upon the Barons, with the result that they published the "Provisions of West-minster"—afterwards enacted as the Statute of Marl-borough.

About this time negotiations between Henry and Louis of France resulted in Henry's renouncing his shadowy claims to Normandy, Anjou and Poitou in return for substantial concessions in Perigord and the Limousin and the reversion of the Agénais. Edward's resentment at the surrender of Normandy led to a renewal of the breach with his father; and private quarrels with Richard de Clare, Earl of Gloucester, threw him on to the side of Simon de Montfort, with whose son Henry the prince had always been on intimate terms. The old king, who had spent the winter in Paris, was alarmed and professed to believe that his son and Earl Simon intended to de-throne him; he insisted upon positive assurances of his son's loyalty before he would return to England, which he eventually did on 25 April 1260, and even then was slow to readmit him to his favour.

It is not improbable that Edward's continued friend-ship with Earl Simon, whose two sons Henry and Simon he knighted this year, was the cause of his being sent out in the autumn to take up his duties as viceroy of Gas-cony. His stay in the province was short, and early in 1261 he returned, visiting several tournaments in France, in which he and his young knights came off badly, losing their horses and arms. Shortly after Edward's return to England, Henry produced a bull from Pope Alexander IV absolving him from the oath which he had taken to observe the Provisions of Oxford; but the prince loyally refused to be released from his obligations in this way, much to his father's annoyance. Later in the year he went over to France, with his brother Edmund, and attended more tournaments, in which he gained wounds and glory; and it seems that at this time he came under the influence of his Poitevin relations and was, by their and his mother's efforts, brought over to his father's side. When he returned to England in March 1263, there was a virtual state of war existing between the king and the Barons, and Edward availed himself of the excuse of his own war in Wales to bring over a contingent of foreign mercenaries. After a futile expedition to the borders of Wales, he placed the greater part of his men in garrison at Windsor and went himself to Bristol. There he failed to gain the city over, and had to call in the aid of the Bishop of Worcester to obtain a safe-conduct to Westminster; on the journey, however, he broke his parole and slipped into Windsor. At the end of June he visited London and broke into the treasury of the New Temple, where he seized £10,000 deposited there for security by various merchants and carried it off to Windsor. When the Barons, bringing King Henry with them, came to besiege the castle, Edward went to confer with them at Kingston, and was arrested; but although his French garrison was expelled from England, he was allowed to retain possession of the castle.

After the rejection by the Barons of King Louis' award, given at Amiens in January 1264, civil war broke out in earnest. Edward was active in the west, and, after taking Brecon from the Welsh and the castles of Hay and Huntingdon from Humphrey de Bohun, advanced on Gloucester. Finding the Barons too strong for him, he obtained a truce for a week, making specious promises of procuring peace on the Barons' terms from the king. Henry de Montfort, against the advice of his companions, took the prince's word and withdrew to Kenilworth. Hardly were the baronial forces out of the town when

Edward, disregarding the truce, plundered the unfortunate burgesses and marched off to join his father at Oxford. Thence, on 3 April, he rode with the royal host to Northampton and was present at the storming of the town, where he saved the life of the younger Simon de Montfort when his captors would have slain him. Edward next led a force westwards into Staffordshire and Derby, taking Tutbury Castle, but hastened back to join the royalist army in the relief of Rochester. Thence they marched into Sussex, down to Winchelsea and westwards to Lewes, which they reached on Sunday, 11 May. Here the King and his retinue quartered themselves in the Priory, while Prince Edward was housed in Earl John de Warenne's strong castle. At Lewes letters were received from the Earls of Leicester and Gloucester expressing loyalty to the King but enmity to his advisers. Edward, rightly seeing himself aimed at in this description, joined with his uncle Richard, now King of the Romans —and very much aware of his own importance—in an answering letter of defiance. Early on the morning of Wednesday, 14 May the Barons had left their camp at Fletching and had gained the heights of the Downs overlooking Lewes on the west. Here they were sighted by a party of foragers, who gave the alarm, and the royalist right wing, under Edward, with the Earls of Surrey and Pembroke, Guy de Lusignan and Hugh Bigod, rapidly took the field. This wing, thrusting its way up the hill near Offham, found itself confronted by the left, and weakest, wing of Montfort's forces, consisting of the London contingent under Nicholas Segrave. Edward's vehement attack shattered the Londoners, who fled in confusion down the slopes to the river and swamps, pursued by the royalists. Glutted with slaughter, the triumphant cavalry turned to plunder the enemy's baggage and when at last Edward brought his men back to the field of battle it was to find his uncle a prisoner, his father shut up in the Priory and their forces broken beyond all hope of recovery. Edward's noble companions cut their way out of the town and fled to Pevensey and so to France, but he refused to desert his father and took shelter in the Franciscan Friary, where he put his seal to the Treaty or Mise of Lewes and surrendered himself as surety for his father's observance of it.

Edward was sent to Dover in custody of Henry de Montfort, and a month later his young consort, Eleanor of Castile, with her baby daughter and her household, were ordered to remove from Windsor to Westminster, whence she later crossed over to France. From Dover the prince was moved later in the year to Wallingford and while he was there a plot to rescue him was made by the royalists who were still holding out on the Welsh march. The attempt was abandoned at Edward's own request, his warders threatening that they would give him up to his friends by hurling him from a mangonel. In December he was in Earl Simon's great castle of Kenilworth, and here he was visited by Mortimer, Clifford and Leyburne, who had been compelled to give up their castles but had apparently received permission to negotiate for his liberation. This was effected, in theory, on 11 March 1265, when Edward was produced publicly in Westminster Hall and after swearing to observe the Great Charters and the regulations recently made for the government of the land, to refrain from any action against the baronial party and to remain in England for three years, was formally handed over to his father. As security he had to make over the fortresses of Dover, Corfe, Nottingham, Scarborough and Bamburgh and to exchange for some of Earl Simon's lands in Leicestershire his palatinate of Chester and the castles of the Peak and Newcastle-under-Lyme. In spite of his theoretical liberation Edward remained in Earl Simon's custody and was taken by him down to Hereford when the Earl found it necessary to move against the Earl of Gloucester, with whom he was now openly at variance. At Hereford, with

the assistance of Thomas de Clare, brother of the Earl of
Gloucester and one of the prince's warders, he got in
touch with his friends and concerted a plan of escape.
On the pretence of trying a number of chargers in order
to select one for use in a tournament he rode out of
Hereford with his keepers on 28 May and after tiring out
their horses mounted a fresh and powerful steed and with
Thomas de Clare and a few other companions galloped
off; Henry de Montfort and his other guards pursued
until they came in sight of a body of armed men under the
banners of Mortimer and Clifford. Passing through
Wigmore, where Roger de Mortimer entertained him,
and Ludlow, Edward rapidly raised a powerful force
with which he fell upon Gloucester early in June, carried
the town in two days and reduced the castle by the end of
the month. Then, hearing from a female spy that the
younger Simon de Montfort was on his way from the
siege of Pevensey and the sack of Winchester to join his
father, the prince led his troops by a forced march from
Worcester and intercepted Simon at Kenilworth in the
early morning of 1 August. The surprise was complete
and decisive. The baronial forces were encamped outside
the castle and kept no watch; they were practically
wiped out, a dozen men of rank being captured and
Simon himself barely managing to escape into the castle.
Edward wasted no time but marched straight back to
Worcester and, hearing that the Earl of Leicester was at
Evesham, set out again at once on the night of 3 August.
Early the next morning the royalist host, with Edward in
the centre and Gloucester and Mortimer on the wings,
came in sight of the enemy. The prince had caused the
banners captured from Montfort's army at Kenilworth
to be carried in front of his troops and it was not until
these were suddenly replaced by the leopards of England,
the chevrons of Gloucester and the blue and gold of
Mortimer that Earl Simon realised that the advancing host
was not that of his son. Prince Edward's generalship had

thus enabled him to effect two surprises in quick succession and his second victory was more complete and overwhelming than the first. From the very beginning the Barons knew that their position was hopeless and there was nothing for them to do but to die bravely. When the battle, or rather butchery, was over Edward gave orders that his fallen adversaries should be buried in the abbey church, and himself attended and mourned over the burial of his old play-fellow Henry de Montfort, but he took no steps to prevent the foul and barbarous mutilation of the great earl's body.

The civil war which might have been brought to a speedy end by the exercise of a little wisdom, was prolonged by Henry's savage desire for revenge. Against the citizens of London he was particularly incensed and he would be satisfied with nothing short of an entire forfeiture of their possessions, which he bestowed upon Edward. Similar severity towards the nobles who had opposed him led to their seizing the Isle of Axholm, against which strong position Edward, who had already taken Dover Castle and compelled the Countess of Leicester and her sons Aumary and Richard to leave the country, was sent in December. As a result of his activities Simon de Montfort came to Northampton under a safe-conduct, which King Henry abused, arresting him and compelling him to swear to surrender Kenilworth and abjure the realm. It is not unlikely that Edward, to whose custody he was committed, condemned this treacherous arrest and connived at his escape, which occurred on 10 February 1266. Simon fled to the Cinque Ports, whose hardy barons were still defying the king and had in the previous November burnt Portsmouth in revenge for Edward's having hanged certain men of Winchelsea and oppressed the citizens of London. Edward was not slow in following Simon and avenging Portsmouth, and on 7 March he attacked and captured Winchelsea. The leader of the portsmen, Henry Pedun, whom he wished to hang out of hand, was saved by the intercession of the Earl of Gloucester and used his influence to bring his fellow barons over. The prince, hearing that a band of outlaws under Sir Adam Gurdon, former Constable of Dunster, were infesting the woods of Alton on the high road to Winchester, then set off to hunt them down. Tradition, picturesque rather than reliable, says that Sir Adam was a famous fighter and that Edward gladly measured his strength against him in single combat, bidding his men stand aside, and after a strenuous combat wounded him, making him first his prisoner and afterwards his faithful servant. From the reduction of isolated bands in the south Edward turned, at the end of June, to the sterner task of besieging Kenilworth Castle. Against this great fortress the entire resources of the royalists proved unavailing until the end of October, when the impossibility of obtaining relief induced the besieged to submit to a compromise by which their personal liberty was guaranteed and they were allowed to compound for their estates. But even yet troubles were not at an end; the Isle of Ely was seized and held by a force of the Disinherited; early in 1267 a rising in the north under John de Vescy was only suppressed by Edward's prompt action and tact; then the Earl of Gloucester occupied London in order to obtain better terms for the defeated party and to force Edward to observe his various oaths and promises. The trouble with Gloucester was composed in the middle of June, and a month later Edward persuaded the barons in Ely to disband on promise of pardon, following up this success by the pacification of the Isle of Wight. Finally, by liberal concessions, Edward obtained peace with Llewelyn, so that by the autumn of 1267 England was at last free from war and the young nobles were able to celebrate the event, and also to expend the remainder of their military ardour, in a series of tournaments under the patronage of Prince Edward and his brother.

Amidst all these troubles a happier note was struck by

the birth, at Windsor on 10 July 1266, of Edward's first son, christened John, the delightful news of which event was brought to King Henry while he was besieging Kenilworth. Another son, Henry, was born in 1268. At this time Edward was contemplating a crusade in the Holy Land and in January had consulted Pope Clement on the subject. The Pope had replied that it would be unwise to leave his aged father so soon after the establishment of peace and while men's minds were still bitter; he also pointed out that Edward could not expect any grant from the English clergy, as they were impoverished by the late troubles and had made a grant of one-tenth to the Barons, in punishment for which the Pope had ordered them to pay another tenth to the king; he might also have alleged the rapacity of his own legate as an additional cause of their impoverishment. However, at the parliament at Northampton on 24 June the Legate Ottobuone preached the crusade with such energy that Edward and Edmund, Henry of Almaine and William de Valence publicly took the cross. Their example was followed by the Earls of Gloucester and Surrey, twenty bannerets and a hundred of the lesser nobility, and the further preaching of the cause in all the towns and boroughs by the friars brought in an innumerable herd of the common people. Preparations for the expedition naturally took time and it was not until August 1269 that Edward was able to go over to France to see King Louis, who was to lead the crusade. It was then arranged that Edward should join Louis in the following August if possible, or in any case should follow as soon as he could, the French king meanwhile advancing him 70,000 pounds of Tours (equivalent to £17,500 sterling) on the security of the revenues of Gascony. As evidence of his good faith Edward on his return to England sent his infant son Henry to King Louis, who with prompt courtesy sent the child back again. Further funds were raised at the parliament held in April 1270 by a grant of a twentieth to be levied on the laity, producing some £30,000. Of this the greater part was paid direct to Edward but part was assigned, at the rate of 100 marks for each knight, to the nobles accompanying him. Thus Henry of Almaine, taking fourteen knights, received 1,500 marks, William de Valence with nineteen knights 2,000 marks, Roger de Leyburne, Roger de Clifford, and Thomas de Clare, each with nine knights, 1,000 marks apiece. An unfortunate quarrel between the Earl of Gloucester and Prince Edward led to the Earl's refusing either to attend parliament or to go on crusade, but was at last compromised by reference to Richard King of the Romans. By his sentence the Earl was to go to the Holy Land, not necessarily with Edward but with the next contingent sailing, and if he would join forces with Edward the king would give him 8,000 marks, but if he would not then he should have only 2,000 marks, which money should be paid when it was known that his ships were actually in the Mediterranean.

At last, on 4 August 1270, Edward took leave of his father, who bestowed on him the cross which he had hoped himself to carry against the pagans, commended his children to the care of his uncle Richard, and moved down to Portsmouth, whence he sailed on 20 August. Hardly had he landed when news arrived of the death of Archbishop Boniface. Leaving his wife and the troops in Gascony, Edward hurried impetuously to Canterbury, thrust his way forcibly into the Chapter-house, where the monks were assembled to elect a new archbishop, and endeavoured to persuade or compel them to elect his chaplain, Robert Brunel. To all his requests and threats they replied firmly that they would not elect anyone whom the Spirit did not inspire them to choose, nor could he even force them to postpone their election. Baffled and angry, the prince retired and once more crossed the sea to Gascony, reaching Aigues Mortes late in September. By this time he must have heard of the death of King Louis at Tunis a month earlier, but he set sail and landed in Tunis. Here he found that Philip, the new King of France, and the other leaders had lost all enthusiasm for the cause and, having obtained a large sum of money from the Sultan, had made peace with him. Edward's indignant protests were met with the reply that the treaty having been made could not be broken, and eventually he agreed to return to Sicily with King Charles and spend the winter there. Accordingly on 20 November the crusading fleet sailed for Sicily, reaching Trapani two days later. The nobles landed at once, leaving their horses, equipment and troops on board, and during the night a great storm arose in which over a hundred large ships, some of them notable for having two masts, were wrecked and the whole of the treasure brought from Tunis was lost, while the English squadron of thirteen ships rode out the storm in safety.

These losses did not make the King of Sicily any the more anxious to resume the enterprise when the winter was over and Edward found that none of the foreign leaders would move; however, he vowed that he would keep his oath at the risk of his life and if none but his groom would go with him yet he would make his way to Acre. Fired by his example all the English contingent, which had been reinforced early in 1271 by the two Edmunds, sons of King Henry and of his brother Richard, vowed to follow him. Early in March Henry of Almaine had obtained leave from Edward to return home, but on his way back he was murdered at Viterbo by Simon and Guy de Montfort: this necessitated the immediate return of his younger brother Edmund, but the remainder of the English crusaders under Edward's leadership left Sicily about mid-Lent and after revictualling at Cyprus reached Acre just in time to save the city, which was on the point of surrendering to the besieging Saracens. Shortly after his arrival Princess Eleanor gave birth to a daughter, who died soon afterwards. Another daughter, Joan "of Acre", was born the following year.

Little else beyond occasional dashing but ineffectual raids, of which the most important resulted in the capture of Nazareth, can be recorded until June 1272. In that month a member of the secret society of the Assassins, fanatics whose name became synonymous with murderers, employed by one of the Emirs in negotiations with Edward obtained a private interview with him under pretence of important secret business and suddenly attacked him with a dagger, wounding him in the arm. Edward repelled him with a vigorous kick and seizing a stool knocked him down and snatched the dagger from him, but in so doing wounded himself in the forehead. The dagger being poisoned, Edward's wounds gave cause for great anxiety; he made his will, appointing executors and guardians for his children, and its very brevity is significant. Popular legend loves to depict the faithful and devoted Eleanor sucking the poison from her husband's arm, but it must regretfully be admitted that in the fullest account by any English contemporary the only reference to Eleanor is less romantic, as the first step taken by the surgeon to whose skill the prince's recovery was attributed was to order the removal of the weeping wife, saying that it was better that she should shed tears than that all England should mourn. Whether Edward owed his life to his wife's devotion, to the medicinal draught administered by the Master of the Templars, to the skill of the ungallant surgeon, or to his own strength of constitution may be questioned, but there is no doubt that the shock of these injuries, coupled with news of his father's failing health and the impossibility of getting reinforcements, led to his concluding a treaty of peace for ten years with the sultan, Bibars, and sailing for Sicily on 15 August. After seven weeks' slow journeying he landed once more at Trapani.

# Chapter Two

# Edward the King

The wearisome journey from Palestine, combined with the strain of crusading life and the actual injuries received at the hands of the murderous Saracen, proved too much for even Edward's splendid constitution, and although he knew of his father's ill health and of the death of his uncle, Richard, King of the Romans, which had occurred on 2 April 1272, Edward made no attempt to hasten to England but remained in Sicily. He was, therefore, at the court of King Charles when news came that King Henry III had died on the evening of 16 November. Edward was an affectionate son and when his royal host expressed surprise that he should show more grief over the death of his father than over the death of his eldest son John in August of the previous year, he replied that children might be replaced but a father could not. Whatever Edward's personal loss, the death of Henry can hardly have been regarded in England as anything but a blessing, and on Sunday, 20 November, the day of Henry's interment in Westminster Abbey, the new reign was formally inaugurated by the Earl of Gloucester publicly swearing fealty and allegiance to King Edward. As Gilbert de Clare, Earl of Gloucester, had been on bad terms with the prince and, although nominally reconciled to him by Richard of Almaine, had managed to avoid going to his assistance in the Holy Land, it was significant that he, of his own free will, should have been the first to come forward and swear allegiance; even if it was an act of

C

mere opportunism, it shows his recognition of the young king's strong position. His example was at once followed by the Archbishop of York and the Earls of Surrey and Hereford and many other nobles. The regency was vested automatically in the Archbishop of York, Roger Mortimer and Robert Burnel, who had been appointed by Edward as his representatives when he left England, and by them the necessary measures were taken for proclaiming the king, ensuring the peace of the country, and summoning a parliament. A week after the death of the old king a formal letter was sent by the prelates and magnates to their new lord informing him of his father's death and desiring him to return to England as soon as possible. Edward's brother Edmund with part of the crusading force hastened home, but Edward remained in Sicily.

In January 1273 a parliament was held at Westminster, at which four knights from each shire and four burgesses from each borough attended and took the oath of allegiance. At the same time Walter of Merton was made Chancellor and it was agreed to suspend the judicial eyres until the king's return, the judges therefore remaining at the central court of King's Bench instead of going on circuit. In the middle of January Edward, in response to an invitation from Pope Gregory X, who as Archdeacon of Liége had accompanied him to the Holy Land, took leave of King Charles and crossed over to the mainland, reaching Rome on 5 February. The papal court was then at Orvieto and there he was welcomed on 14 February with great honour and magnificence. He at once brought pressure to bear upon the Pope to secure the punishment of Guy de Montfort for the murder of Henry of Almaine. Although Henry had been butchered at the very altar in the church of Viterbo by his cousins Simon and Guy the criminals had been left unpunished, through the influence of Guy's father-in-law Count Aldobrandini il Rosso. Simon was now dead but Edward was able to persuade the Pope to call Guy to account, and before he left Orvieto at the beginning of June he had the satisfaction of knowing that Guy had been excommunicated and outlawed and his lands placed under interdict, in spite of the intervention of his brother Aumary de Montfort, who was a papal chaplain. Some six months later Guy submitted himself unreservedly to the Pope and was committed to prison, where he remained for ten years; after this he served for four years in the papal forces but was then captured by Roger di Loria, the Arragonese admiral, and imprisoned by Edward's influence until his death.

About the beginning of June 1273 Edward left the papal court and made his way northwards. The fame which he had won in the crusades converted his journey into a triumphal progress; at every city he was received with acclamations and processions, and at Milan the citizens presented him with a number of chosen chargers caparisoned in scarlet trappings, which he accepted with a becoming show of unwillingness. On 7 June he reached the pass of Mont Cenis, and as he descended the mountains he was met by a party of English nobles with the Bishops of Winchester and Exeter, who had started a month earlier, expecting to meet the king in Paris. He was also welcomed by Philip, Count of Savoy, who as Bishop-elect of Lyons had entertained him in 1260, and, as his health was again bad, he spent some time at the count's castle of St. George near Vienne. Here on 25 June he received the count's homage for the fortress of Bard, and about the same time William de Tournon, an independent baron who had used his stronghold on the Rhône to plunder passers-by and had even taken toll of Edward's stores when he was on his way to Aigues Mortes, deemed it wise to make his peace with the king by becoming his man. Shortly afterwards Edward with a large body of knights moved up to Chalons, the count of which place had challenged him to joust. As a king and a crusader Edward ought not to have taken part in a tournament but it was a form of sport to which he was always addicted and the challenge conveyed a reflection on his personal prowess which he was quick to resent. Unlike the formal jousting of a later date such a tournament as this was a confused engagement between two bodies of knights, of which even the numbers were not equal, the count having considerably more men than the king. The two leaders soon sought each other out and indulged in a prolonged bout of sword-play, till the count, finding that he had met his match, suddenly dropped his sword and flung his arms round Edward's neck, trying to drag him off his horse. The tall king straightened himself and spurring his horse galloped forward with his adversary clinging to him. When he had lifted the count clear of his horse and had borne him a little distance Edward flung him off violently and rode out of the press to recover his breath. Resting a moment and looking round he saw that the Burgundian bystanders were attacking and plundering the English; bidding his men avenge themselves on their assailants, which they were quick to do, he returned to the fray and seeking out the shaken count, who had been remounted by his friends, gave him a good drubbing and compelled him to yield. This finished the "Little Battle of Chalons", as the tournament was called from the bloodshed involved, save that, owing to his men being assaulted in the streets, Edward had to secure the peace by informing the mayor and provosts that if they did not punish the offenders he would burn the town to the ground.

From Chalons King Edward went to Paris, which he reached about 17 July. Here he was received with apparent friendliness by King Philip III. The two kings were first cousins and professed affection for each other, though, as a contemporary chronicler observes, it was the love of a cat for a dog. Queen Eleanor, who had been on a visit to her brother at Seville in June but had rejoined her husband at the end of that month, did not accompany him to Paris but went by easy stages towards Bayonne. On 26 July she reached Limoges, where she was received with much splendour by the burgesses, who made a feast in her honour and begged her to persuade King Edward to help them against the oppression of their Viscountess. By the treaty of 1259 Limoges should have been ceded to Henry III. Accordingly Edward sent troops under his seneschal to assist the burgesses, and on 7 August, the day on which he left Paris after having done homage to Philip "for all the lands which he ought to hold of him", these troops gained a considerable victory over the army of the Viscountess. Following up this success Edward caused the men of Limoges to take an oath of fealty to William de Valence, his deputy; this was done, but King Philip sent an order to Edward to renounce the oath and to cease molesting the Viscountess. Meanwhile King Edward was slowly making his way down to Bayonne, reducing to order the independent barons of Gascony and in particular carrying on a little war with the restless Gaston, Vicomte de Béarn, father-in-law of the murdered Henry of Almaine. Gaston was captured at the end of September and compelled to surrender the town and castle of Orthez and to swear not to leave the king's court without his permission, one of the four sureties for his observance of his oath being Sir Arnald de Gaveston, father of the afterwards notorious Piers. Immediately after extorting this submission from Gaston at Sault Edward met Pedro, the heir to the throne of Aragon, at Sordes and drew up an agreement by which the eldest daughter of the English king was to marry the eldest son of the Spanish prince. A month later Edward negotiated another marriage between his infant son Henry and Joan daughter of Henry, King of Navarre and Count of Champagne and Brie; but neither match was destined to be performed. A week before the signing of the second marriage contract, on 24 November 1273, Queen Eleanor had given birth to a son at Bayonne. He was christened Alphonso, after his uncle the King of Spain, who in his own person acted as sponsor.

Gaston de Béarn, adopting the tactics once successfully employed by his royal captor, had galloped away from his keepers and for some months defied Edward, carrying on a sort of guerrilla warfare of raids and plundering. After wasting much time and money to little purpose both parties agreed to submit their dispute to their over-lord the King of France. Edward's intention of returning to England for his coronation at Easter 1274 was, how-ever, defeated by a letter from the Pope requesting him to postpone the ceremony so that it should not clash with the General Council which he had summoned to meet at Lyons on 1 May. For nearly seven weeks the Council sat and debated on the question of renewing the crusade. The envoys of the Tartars offered to accept Christianity, the representatives of the Greek Church were willing to renounce their opinions on "the procession of the Holy Ghost" and be reunited to the Roman Church, the clergy of Europe submitted to the payment of a tenth of their incomes for six years to the cause, but neither Edward nor any other military leader would move a hand or send a soldier. During these seven weeks Edward had spent most of his time in the neighbourhood of Limoges. He entered that city on 8 May and was received in procession by the monks of St. Martial. Two days later he met a deputation of the clergy urging the avoidance of war with the Viscountess and also gave audience to the proctors of Gaston de Béarn. On both matters King Philip had for-bidden him to proceed and he therefore sent messengers to the French court and spent the next five weeks hunting in the neighbourhood, returning briefly to the city for the feast of Whitsun. His messengers eventually returned empty-handed and to the burgesses who begged him to assist them Edward could only give a reluctant refusal, not wishing to offend Philip. At last, on 7 June, the men of Limoges made one final appeal, flinging the keys of their city at his feet and imploring him to save them. Much moved, Edward undertook to go in person to the French king and set off for Paris, leaving a force of English soldiers, to be employed only for defensive purposes; in the course of the next month, however, they were led by William de Valence against Aixe and Edward's chief engineer was set to make machines for casting fire into the town. Before the siege could be brought to a successful conclusion orders came from King Philip that both parties were to cease fighting and refer their quarrel to his next parliament. At this parliament decision was given that King Edward had no rights in Limoges, and for the injuries done to Aixe he was cast in damages to the amount of £22,600—of the payment of which there appears to be no record. At this same parliament Gaston de Béarn denounced Edward, who by this time had crossed over to England, as a traitor and flung down the gauntlet of defiance. The challenge was accepted on Edward's behalf by Sir William de Valence, Sir Aumary de Rochechouart, and other knights, but Gaston refused to fight any of them and, failing to sustain his case, was condemned by Philip, who seized his lands and sent him over to Edward. After further delays and appeals Gaston was reconciled to the king in 1276 and gave no more trouble.

At Paris Edward met Henry le Waleys, Mayor of London, Gregory de Rokesle, and Luke de Batencurt, sent by the city at his request to consult with him about the trouble with Flanders which had broken out in the spring of 1274. The aggressive actions of the Countess Margaret had driven Edward to forbid the export of wool to Flanders and to seize the ships of Flemish merchants. These measures soon compelled the Flemings to come to terms and Margaret's son, Count Guy, met Edward at Montreuil, near Boulogne, on 28 July and agreed to peace on the terms of mutual indemnification for injuries inflicted by their respective subjects. Investigation showed a balance of nearly £5,000 due to the English merchants, which was still unpaid in December 1276. After his interview with Count Guy there was nothing more to delay King Edward's return to England, and at last, on Thursday, 2 August 1274 he set foot as king on the shores of his native land, which he had quitted as prince just four years earlier.

The first official document which passed his hand after his landing appears to have been an order for the payment of money for the expenses of the royal children, Eleanor, Henry, and the infant Alphonso, who had preceded his parents, arriving in London on 14 June; the fourth surviving child, Joan of Acre, had been entrusted to her grandmother, the Countess of Ponthieu. Being unwilling to enter London until all things were ready for the coronation the king moved up from Dover, where he had landed, slowly, spending a few days at Canterbury and then staying with the Earl of Gloucester at Tonbridge and with John de Warenne, Earl of Surrey, at Reigate. It was on Saturday, 18 August, that Edward reached London, where he was received with great magnificence and enthusiasm by the citizens, who concealed, if they had not forgotten, their former enmity towards him. Preparations had been made on a vast scale: all the vacant spaces within the court of Westminster were covered with temporary buildings; to the south of the palace were several great halls containing solid tables at which the magnates and all who would, rich or poor, might feast on the day of the coronation and for the fortnight following. Elsewhere the blue smoke was pouring up out of the open roof of the great roasting kitchen and, as even the number of auxiliary kitchens erected was not sufficient, cooking places had been hastily constructed in the open. For the employment of all these hearths prodigious supplies of provisions had been prepared; the original orders sent out to the sheriffs of various counties for live-stock amount to over a thousand pigs, five hundred oxen, two hundred and fifty sheep and the almost incredible number of twenty-seven thousand chickens, as well as indefinite numbers of such dainties as swans, peacocks, cranes, salmon, eels and lampreys. The whole palace had been done up, the halls whitewashed and painted, and the paths from the palace to the Abbey carpeted with cloth from the looms of Candlewick Street (now Cannon Street). Along these carpeted ways Edward and Eleanor walked in procession, beneath silken canopies hung with silver bells, on the following day, Sunday, 19 August, to the great Abbey church, at whose dedication after its rebuilding by the old King Henry they had been present on 13 October 1269. In the procession, with the magnates of England, were Alexander III of Scotland, and John of Brittany, with their wives, King Edward's sisters. After the ceremony of consecration and coronation, at which Robert Kilwardby, Archbishop of Canterbury, officiated, the royal procession returned to the palace for the banquet and all London, in its gayest clothes, gave itself up to feasting and merriment, to which the conduit in Cheapside, flowing all day with white wine and red, lent its assistance. In Westminster Hall, a blaze of silk and cloth of gold, attention centred on the commanding figure of the king and the youthful beauty of his queen as they sat at the high table clad in their royal robes and wearing their crowns. Near them were the king's two fair sisters, Margaret of Scotland and Beatrice of Brittany, and the little Prince Henry, wearing a chaplet of flowers, all three destined to die within the year.

King Edward was well fitted to be the central figure in this scene of magnificence. In the prime of life, at the beginning of his thirty-sixth year, he seemed marked out by nature to be a king; tall beyond the common lot of man and powerfully built, with broad chest and nervous arms and legs whose unusual length gained him the nickname of "Longshanks" and gave him a seat on horseback from which, as the Count of Chalons had learnt to his cost, he could not easily be dislodged. His hair, once flaxen, had darkened almost to blackness, his forehead was broad and his features regular, save that the left eyelid drooped noticeably, as his father's had done. A slight stammer which affected his speech was counteracted by his skilful use of words. And these outward characteristics were to an unusual extent the expression of the man himself. If a slight mental stammer made him occasionally depart from the strict letter of his promise and go back upon his word, yet his general honesty and largeness of mind tempt us to excuse an occasional lapse. And as the fair hair of boyhood had darkened and the immature defeated jouster of 1260 had developed into the strong champion of Christendom, so the fiery impetuosity of the prince had sobered down into the controlled, unflinching determination of the king. His experiences in the Barons' War and later in Palestine had given him a training, moral as well as military, by which he had not failed to profit and alike as a general and a statesman he did more than gain fame; he deserved it. In private life he was a faithful and affectionate husband and if we know little of him as a father he was certainly a dutiful son, grieving over his father's death and treating his widowed mother with loving courtesy. That his affection did not blind him may be gathered from a story told of a visit paid by him to his mother after she had taken the veil at Amesbury. On this occasion she told him of a miracle alleged to have been worked by the virtue of the dead King Henry, a man who had long been blind having recovered his sight at the king's tomb. It so happened that Edward knew the man for a liar and a knave and he tried to persuade his mother not to believe the story; the credulous and querulous old lady broke into reproaches and bade him leave her room; as he withdrew he met a friar to whom he told the tale, adding:—"I know my father's sense of justice, that he would more likely have torn the eyes out of such a scoundrel than have restored vision to the reprobate." In religious matters Edward might be called business-like; if he lacked the excessive and embarrassing piety of his father and did not hesitate to challenge the claims of the Church when they conflicted with those of the State, yet on the other hand he was far removed from the careless impiety of Henry II. He neither neglected religion nor allowed it to interfere with his policy; he was, to misuse a favourite eighteenth-century commendation, "religious without enthusiasm", and his attitude finds expression in his action in the Scottish war at the end of his reign, when, requiring lead for his military machines, he ordered that it should be taken from the roofs of churches but that the portion of the roof over the sanctuary should not be stripped. Stern in opposition, he could be merciful in victory, and if he extorted money on an unprecedented scale it was not for the enrichment of favourites but for objects of policy which he considered to be in the interests of his subjects, to whom he endeavoured to ensure prosperity and justice. Such a man the thirty-five years of his reign were to show Edward to be, but on that August day as he sat at the high table in Westminster Hall it was no doubt upon his manly bearing and military prowess that most minds were fixed.

The day after the coronation Edward received the homage of the magnates, including that of King Alexander, not however for his realm of Scotland but solely for his English lands. At the same time Edward's brother Edmund renounced his claim to the Stewardship of England, which had been bestowed upon him by King Henry with Simon de Montfort's earldom of Leicester and which he had exercised at the coronation; the office was then restored to him for life. There seems to have been at this time a slight coolness between the two brothers over the question of their crusading expenses. While at Orvieto Edward had obtained from the Pope a grant of three years' tenths from the English clergy towards his expenses; but almost at the same time the papal commissioners in England had arranged that the clergy should pay two years' tenths, one to Edward and one to Edmund. King Edward, who was heavily in debt to the Italian merchants who had acted as his bankers, was unwilling to give up any of the money on which he had reckoned; Edmund was equally unwilling to relinquish his share and the Pope found it necessary to write to the brothers and to their mother urging an amicable arrangement. If there was still any ill-feeling between them they must soon have been reunited in affliction by a series of losses. The little Prince Henry, whose health had given cause for anxiety on several occasions, fell seriously ill not long after his father's coronation; the skill of his medical attendants proved unavailing and the aid of the saints was invoked in vain, wax candles of the length of his body being sent to burn before the shrines of St. Thomas at Canterbury and St. Edward at Westminster, as also before the tomb of his grandfather King Henry, and at the altars of St. James at Reading, St. Fromund at Dunstable, and St. Momartre outside Guildford; on 14 October he died. Within a month Edmund's wife, Aveline de Forz, died, to his great sorrow, and in the spring of 1275 the royal sisters Margaret of Scotland and Beatrice of Brittany died within a few weeks of each other. About the same time Edward's aunt, Eleanor widow of Simon de Montfort, to whom he had become reconciled during his stay in Paris, also died.

# Chapter Three

# Establishing his Authority

Although Edward's accession had been undisputed the absence of the king from England for two years, following on the eclipse of the monarchy during the last years of the reign of Henry III, had not been without its effect. Early in 1273 there had been a rising, anarchical and aimless, in the north; Robert de Ferrers, the restless Earl of Derby, had seized Chartley Castle in Staffordshire and had had to be brought to order by a force under Edmund of Lancaster and the Earl of Lincoln; while in Yorkshire the sheriff had fought something like a pitched battle with a lawless band led by Walter Dewyas. In October of the same year the new Archbishop of Canterbury, Robert Kilwardby, solemnly excommunicated all disturbers of the peace; in February 1274 the king had instructed the regency council to call a meeting of magnates, significantly ordering them to summon those who would do what was required rather than those of great rank or wealth; and in May there were rumours of an attempt to seize the Isle of Ely, that favourite Cave of Adullam for the discontented, and the bishop was ordered to sink all boats on the shores of the island and to keep careful watch, day and night. If these incidents could hardly be considered as seriously menacing King Edward's position yet they were significant of a general state of unrest and we might assume, even without the abundant corroborative evidence which exists, that disorder was prevalent in the land and that, by an inevitable corollary, the poorer inhabitants were suffering at the hands of their superiors. Such a state of affairs was abhorrent to King Edward, who combined an exceptional sympathy, or at least tolerance, for his humbler subjects with an autocratic distrust of the greater lords. To restore order, do justice to the poor, and check the power of the nobles was one of the first tasks which the king undertook on his return. With these aims in view he appointed Robert Burnel, upon whom he could absolutely rely, Chancellor in September 1274, compensating Walter de Merton, who had filled that office faithfully down to the coronation, with the vacant bishopric of Rochester. During the next three months the greater number of the sheriffs were removed from office and replaced by others, and on 11 October orders were sent out for a general enquiry into a variety of abuses throughout the kingdom. The details of this great inquest will be dealt with in another chapter; here it will be sufficient to say that the returns showed innumerable encroachments upon the royal prerogatives and a vast amount of cruelty and oppression by landowners and officials, and still more by their subordinates. Even more menacing than the isolated outbreaks and general lawlessness was the attitude of the Welsh. Immediately after the death of Henry III the abbots of Dore and Haghmond had been sent to the Welsh frontier at Montgomery to receive Llewelyn's fealty to King Edward, but the Welsh prince had simply ignored their summons. Llewelyn's previous encounters with Edward had not been of a kind to inspire him with much respect for the English king. For five years, from 1256 to 1260, the Welsh had defied the English successfully. Edward had been obliged to abandon the attempt to tame them and had had to be content with maintaining a defensive attitude against them. Then, after the defeat of Montfort's party, to which he had been allied, Llewelyn had obtained terms so favourable compared with those granted to the English barons that he was justified in believing that the English feared him. Unfortunately for himself he was moved by this belief to throw off the light yoke of nominal vassalage to the English crown and assume the status of an independent king. Edward was not the man to acquiesce in such an attitude and on 3 November 1274 he sent from Northampton, where he was staying, a peremptory demand that Llewelyn should meet him at Shrewsbury and render his homage. Llewelyn evaded the direct demand by feigning to believe that it would be unsafe for him to come to Shrewsbury and the question of the homage was temporarily shelved by Edward's falling ill, the poison still lingering in his wounds having led to the formation of an abscess.

After resting ten days at Kings Cliffe and another ten days at the neighbouring royal manor of Geddington, the king was sufficiently recovered to make his way to Woodstock, where he kept Christmas. January 1275 Edward spent in Wiltshire and Hampshire, after which he was at Windsor for six weeks. During this spring the question of a renewal of the crusade was raised in several quarters. To Abaga Khan, Prince of the Moguls, who had assumed Christianity out of enmity towards the Saracens, Edward wrote commending his action and his intention of invading Palestine, committing the Christians in the Holy Land to his care, but holding out only shadowy hopes of any assistance. To Alphonso of Castile, now King of the Romans, who desired his help against the Moors, he replied that he had already been asked by the Pope whether he would go to the aid of the Holy Land and was still considering what he ought to do; meanwhile, though he could not himself come to Alphonso's assistance, he would be very willing for his subjects in Bayonne to give their help, and he followed up this offer by sending letters to the Mayor of Bayonne and others for ships to be provided to serve against the Moors. A great parliament, at which the commons as well as the magnates appear to have been represented, had been summoned for

22 April but, as Edward was at Wallingford on that date
and did not reach Westminster till two days later, it is
probable that it did not meet until about the 26th. At
this parliament was passed the First Statute of Westminster, which was practically a codification of the law
on a great variety of subjects, from the extortion of
feudal aids to the control of elections, including the procedure against criminous clerks. With its details we deal
elsewhere, but its general effect was equivalent to a
declaration that the king intended to see that justice was
done to all classes of his subjects. By way of reminding
his subjects that the crown was entitled to some substantial recognition of its benevolence Edward obtained
a grant of a customs duty of 6s. 8d. on each sack of wool
(worth about £6) or 300 wool-fells exported and 13s. 4d.
on each last of hides.

At the beginning of August the court moved to Oxford, where the king was welcomed with great joy;
although there were not many students in residence at the
time the townspeople made up for their absence. They
came out to meet the king and queen in crowds, the
women dressed in their handsomest clothes and carrying
large tapers, and the town was gaily decorated; but their
trouble was thrown away, for the king would not ride
through the gay streets. There was a legend that no king
might enter the town of Oxford under the penalty of
St. Frideswide's displeasure; Henry III alone had infringed the saint's prohibition, and then only after an
elaborate preparation of deprecatory prayer. Edward had
been present when his father entered Oxford in the spring
of 1264 and had possibly felt that the disastrous Battle of
Lewes, which had followed in little more than a month,
was at least an unpleasant coincidence; whatever his
reasons, he preferred to bow to the superstition and avoid
all risk by remaining outside the walls, as Henry II had
done at Lincoln, to which city a similar legend was attached. It was therefore at Beaumont and not within the

town that Edward interviewed Gaston de Béarn and committed him to the custody of Sir Stephen de Pencestre. From Oxford King Edward moved on for a few days to his favourite palace of Woodstock, whence he wrote on 12 August to the prelates and barons of Ireland urging them to consult as to the best means of putting an end to the interminable quarrels and factions by which the island was vexed and impoverished. Next he made his way northwards to Chester, where he remained for the first ten days of September waiting for Llewelyn to come and render his homage. As the Welsh prince failed to appear, Edward sent him a peremptory summons to attend at Westminster within three weeks of Michaelmas. For the same date, 13 October 1275, a second parliament was convened to which knights of the shire, representatives of the counties, were summoned. Llewelyn declined to attend this parliament on the ground that his life would be in danger if he ventured into England; he said that he had not forgotten the death of his father Gruffudd, who fell from the Tower of London and was found with his neck broken, and then demanded as hostages if he came the king's son, the Earl of Gloucester and the Chancellor, Robert Burnel, for whom Edward had obtained the bishopric of Bath earlier in the year. Edward's reply to this insolent demand was to persuade parliament to grant him a fifteenth of all moveable goods, chiefly for the expenses of a war with Wales, which he now saw was inevitable, though its actual outbreak was postponed.

The second half of January 1276 was spent by Edward at Winchester where he composed a quarrel of long standing between the citizens and again gave audience to Gaston de Béarn, with whom he now became reconciled, only stipulating that he should make such amends as King Philip might decree. About the same time Edmund of Lancaster married the beautiful and wealthy Blanche of Artois, widow of King Henry of Navarre. The French King's guardianship of Jeanne, heir to the

D

throne of Navarre, coupled with his support of his
nephews in their claim to be recognised as the nearest
heirs in the succession of Castile, led to war between
Alphonso of Castile and Philip of France, and both
parties appealed to Edward for assistance. While his
sympathies were on the side of his brother-in-law
Alphonso, he had to refuse to help him, as such action
would involve fighting his feudal over-lord the King of
France. On the other hand he was unwilling to obey
Philip's demand for his services, though justified by that
overlordship, as he would then have to fight against
Alphonso, at whose hands he had received the honour of
knighthood. In the circumstances he acknowledged his
duty to Philip but expressed the hope that he might be of
use by mediating rather than by fighting, and arranged
to go over to France in November. But by this time the
state of affairs in Wales afforded him an excuse for post-
poning his visit. Llewelyn had been summoned to meet
the king at Winchester in January but had ignored the
summons. Shortly after this a small squadron of ships
from Bristol captured off the Scilly Isles the ship on which
Eleanor, daughter of Simon de Montfort, was on her
way to marry Llewelyn. With her was a small escort
under her brother Aumary, the papal chaplain who had
defended Guy de Montfort on the charge of murdering
Henry of Almaine. Aumary had tried to cross to England
some two years earlier by attaching himself to his father's
old friend Stephen de Berkestede, Bishop of Chichester,
when the bishop was in Paris on his way back from the
papal court. The only result had been that the men of the
Cinque Ports had been ordered to fit out ships to prevent
either the bishop or Aumary landing and a spy had been
sent to keep watch on their movements in Paris. Edward
had soon been reconciled to Bishop Stephen, and indeed
on 16 June 1276 he was present at Chichester with a
crowd of nobles when the bishop translated the body of
his predecessor St. Richard de Wyche to the new shrine

prepared for its reception, but against Aumary his feelings were still bitter. He was also naturally delighted to have in his hands the Welsh prince's affianced bride, and he showed his pleasure by a gift of 100s. to the bringer of the good news and by the distribution of no less than £90 to the crews of the ships which had effected the capture. Eleanor was committed to honourable custody at Windsor, two Welsh priests with her were sent to Beaulieu and the remainder of her escort, after some months' strict imprisonment at Bristol, were allowed to abjure the realm, but Aumary remained in prison at Corfe and afterwards in Sherborne Castle.

Llewelyn, having been summoned again to a parliament at Westminster in October 1276, so far condescended as to offer to do homage to the king at Montgomery or Oswestry on certain conditions. As these conditions included a safe-conduct guaranteed by the Archbishop of Canterbury and five earls—a distinct reflection on Edward's unsupported word—and the surrender of Eleanor and her companions, whom he offered to ransom, the king's council, before whom they were laid in November, declined to consider them and gave orders for an army to be called together for service against Llewelyn. Edward, however, wished to avoid war if possible and in any case was unwilling to risk a Welsh campaign in winter; the date for the assembling of the army at Worcester was therefore fixed for Midsummer 1277 and meanwhile the prelates brought pressure to bear upon the prince. Their threats of excommunication were ignored by Llewelyn, who refused even to admit their messengers to his presence, and accordingly in March he was denounced as excommunicate. It will be more satisfactory to treat the military operations of all Edward's Welsh campaigns together in a separate chapter and it is therefore sufficient to say here that between July and November 1277 Edward, without fighting any pitched battle of importance, reduced his adversary to terms.

On 9 November Llewelyn set his seal to a treaty by which he admitted the overlordship of King Edward and bound himself to pay £50,000 as indemnity for his rebellion. He surrendered the four cantreds, corresponding roughly to the counties of Flint and Denbigh, which had been made over to him in 1267 and all the districts conquered by Edward, receiving back Anglesey as a fief to be held by himself and the heirs of his body of the English crown at a rent of 1,000 marks, and the district of Snowdon. The king reserved to himself the homage of all the Welsh lords, with the exception of five barons of Snowdon whose homage was left to Llewelyn for his life but would revert to the English King on his death, so that the title of prince would then expire, a prince without vassals being inconceivable. Finally, Llewelyn was to release his brother Owen and other political prisoners, to find hostages for his observance of the treaty, and to do fealty and homage to Edward. Next day the Welsh prince came from Conway to Rhuddlan and swore fealty to King Edward, who remitted the fine of £50,000, which there was no possibility of his ever paying, and the 1,000 marks rent for Anglesey. The reception of his homage was postponed till he had been reconciled to the Church, and it was eventually rendered at Westminster, where he remained at the court for Christmas.

The parliament of October 1276, Llewelyn's absence from which had been the cause of the Welsh war, passed two Acts of some importance. Of these the Statute *De Bigamis* was practically a recognition of the decree of the Council of Lyons by which a clerk marrying a second time or contracting a union with a widow lost the benefit of his clergy and became amenable to the lay courts if indicted of felony. The Statute of Rageman authorised a general enquiry by the Justices Itinerant into the acts of corruption and oppression by officials, particularly the sheriffs, during the last twenty years. This was followed by the removal of almost all the sheriffs, most of whom were royal officials appointed when the king first came to England, and their replacement by men of local influence and interest. A start was thus made to remedy the abuses revealed in the enquiry of 1275. Another abuse, the growth of money-lending and usury, was also dealt with; orders being issued in December 1276 for an enquiry as to Christians who were behaving like Jews in practising usury, which was forbidden by canon and civil law to members of the Faith, and had been forbidden, ineffectually, to the Jews in an Act passed in 1275. At the same time measures were to be taken against both Jews and Christians who were guilty of the practice of clipping coins, a process to which the thin irregular silver pennies lent themselves temptingly. The year 1277 was so much occupied with the Welsh war that little of more than local importance has been recorded; even the weather was unusually normal and there were none of the great storms, frosts, earthquakes or celestial phenomena in which the contemporary chroniclers delighted. During 1278 Edward was much engaged with family and foreign affairs; early in January Queen Eleanor had given birth to a child, which does not seem to have lived. In the same month envoys came from John, Duke of Brabant, to negotiate for the marriage of his son with Edward's daughter Margaret. She was at this time two years old and was his only unaffianced daughter, Eleanor's hand having been promised to the son of the King of Aragon and Joan of Acre being destined for Hartman, son of Rudolph of Hapsburg, King and afterwards Emperor of the Romans. Negotiations for the marriage with Hartman had been begun in 1276 and the ceremony had at first been fixed for the spring of 1278. Its postponement may have been due to the request of Edward's aunt, the Dowager Queen Margaret of France, that he would not allow it to take place while Rudolph was at war with the Count of Savoy; at any rate in May 1278 Rudolph authorised Edward to make peace on his behalf with the count; and in the following month Edward sent Sir Stephen de Pencestre and Margaret his wife to bring back Joan from her grandmother Joan of Castile, in whose care she had been for the past four or five years. In November he wrote to the Bishop of Verdun, asking him to come over for the wedding of Joan and Hartman. In April 1279 arrangements were again made for Hartman to come over, but again his visit was postponed and the marriage had not been performed when the young prince was accidentally drowned by the breaking of the ice on which he was skating in 1282.

On 17 January 1278 King Edward left London and made his way slowly down to Dover, where he stayed for two weeks, sending Stephen de Pencestre and Anthony Bek to France as his proctors to receive the Agénais, the cession of which was due under the treaty of 1259. At the same time he wrote to King Philip, as he had already done six months before, protesting against his attempting to reopen the whole case between himself and Gaston de Béarn when his part was only to fix what amends Gaston should make. By the end of March the king was at Downampney in Gloucestershire, and from there he wrote to his trusted agents Burnel and Otes de Graundson expressing his approval of their actions at the French court and his confidence in them, warning them to bind the shifty Gascons to their promises by as many guarantees as possible, and informing them that Llewelyn was behaving obediently and that King Alexander of Scotland intended to come and render homage at London at Michaelmas. Two or three days later he received the papal messengers sent to announce the election of Giovanni Gaetano Orsini as pope, under the title of Nicholas III. For Easter, 17 April, the court was at Glastonbury and while there the king caused the traditional tomb of King Arthur, within the precincts of the Abbey, to be opened and his bones to be removed to the treasury of the monastery until such time as a fit

resting place could be prepared for them. May and June
were spent at Westminster, the king going on 29 May
to Lambeth to attend the consecration of the new bishops
of Norwich and Rochester, the latter see being vacant by
the death of the famous ex-Chancellor Walter of Merton
from the effects of being thrown off his horse into the
water. The ceremony was performed by Robert Kilwardby
and was almost his last act as Archbishop of Canterbury,
as he was shortly afterwards removed from the primacy
by Pope Nicholas and given a cardinalate and the
bishopric of Porto. The see of Canterbury being thus
left vacant, the monks, more subservient to Edward as
king than they had been to him as prince, elected the
Chancellor, Robert Burnel, Bishop of Bath and Wells.
Edward had no fear that Burnel would follow the
precedent of Becket and change from a loyal chancellor
into a pugnacious champion of the Church, and he
accordingly sent an influential embassy, headed by his
secretary, the famous Bolognese lawyer Francesco dei
Accursi, to the Pope with a letter of extravagant praise
for Burnel as the man of all English prelates and clerks
most dear to him. Nicholas, however, had as little hope
as Edward had fear of Burnel proving a second Becket
and declined to subject the English Church to one who
was officially the king's mouthpiece and in his private
life practically a layman. Burnel was therefore rejected
and the vacant primacy was filled by the appointment of
John Pecham, a Franciscan friar of unblemished character
and world-wide reputation for learning.

During the year a careful watch had been kept on
Llewelyn and his behaviour had been so far correct that
Edward now felt justified in allowing his marriage with
Eleanor de Montfort to take place. During August and
September, therefore, the king made a leisurely progress
through the border counties from Gloucester to Rhudd-
lan, returning by Macclesfield and Stafford to Worcester.
On 17 September he gave orders for the ten Welsh

hostages to be sent back to Llewelyn and the prince acknowledged his courtesy a few days later by sending gifts of four hunting dogs to the king and two greyhounds to the queen. At Worcester on 13 October the marriage of Llewelyn and Eleanor took place in the presence of King Edward, who provided the wedding fee of a mark of silver which was placed on the missal with the wedding ring, and of Queen Eleanor, who presented the bride with a costly kerchief. It is probable that King Alexander of Scotland was also present at the ceremony, as he was certainly at Tewkesbury a few days later, when he offered to do homage to King Edward; the homage, however, was postponed on the ground that the royal council was not present, and it was therefore performed at the autumn parliament at Westminster. In his letter to Burnel earlier in the year Edward had characterised the homage to be tendered as "unconditional" and it is noticeable that the actual phrase employed—"I, Alexander King of Scotland, become the liege man of the lord Edward King of England, against all men"—contained no definition of the lands for which the homage was due, thus leaving the question of the suzerainty of England over Scotland open. The oath of fealty which was sworn on Alexander's behalf by Robert Bruce, Earl of Carrick, also vaguely promised fealty to Edward for "the lands which I hold of the said King of England"—practically the same non-committal formula as Edward himself had used in doing fealty to King Philip.

After the autumn parliament of 1278 had come to an end, in the middle of November, the court left Westminster and the king and queen were at Norwich on the first Sunday in Advent, 26 November, for the dedication of the cathedral. In the last year of the reign of Henry III the friction between the monks of the cathedral priory and the townsmen of Norwich had produced an explosion of unusual violence culminating in an attack upon the priory in the course of which part of the cathedral had been burnt. The usual lengthy process of accusations and refutations, appeals and counter-appeals, had ended in favour of the monks in 1275, when Edward had ordered the citizens to pay 3,000 marks damages, in yearly instalments of 500 marks, and also to make a gold ciborium of the value of £100 for the high altar; at the same time the citizens were released from the sentences of excommunication and interdict under which they lay. The damage to the cathedral had now been made good and the presence of King Edward at the consecration service no doubt emphasised his intention to deal severely with those who infringed the liberties of the Church with unauthorised violence. Meanwhile his hand had fallen heavily upon the Church's traditional enemies the Jews. In the recent parliament attention seems to have been directed to the serious injury being inflicted upon the coinage, and therefore upon national credit, by the wide-spread practice of clipping and cutting the currency. The only English coin in circulation at this time was the silver penny, a disc of silver about the size of a modern sixpence but thinner, and of only approximate roundness. The clipping of small pieces of metal from the edges of these coins was a tempting and profitable form of crime and the fact that halfpence and farthings were formed by cutting the penny into halves or quarters encouraged the evil practice, which had grown to such an extent that the currency had lost from ten to fifteen per cent of its weight and had naturally become unacceptable to foreign merchants. As the Jews were preeminently associated with money transactions suspicion inevitably fell upon them, and on 18 November a general order was issued for the arrest throughout the country of all Jews suspected of coin-clipping. Six hundred Jews were seized and sent up to the Tower and a considerable number of Christians, especially goldsmiths, were also arrested. Special justices were appointed to try the prisoners, but their sessions were suspended during Lent and on their

resumption after Easter, 2 April 1279, it was found that
money was being extorted from the Jews still at large by
threats of accusation and arrest. Edward at once forbade
such actions and ordered that those Jews who had not
been accused before the first of May should not be
molested; but, as usual, tempering justice with parsimony,
he added the condition that they should pay a fine for
their immunity. In the end some 290 Jews were executed
in London, and possibly others may have been put to
death elsewhere, while very many were fined; of the
Christian offenders only two or three paid the penalty in
their persons but many suffered in their purses. The
total value of goods forfeited and the fines extracted in
this connexion seems to have been approximately
£10,000. To prevent the recurrence of coin-clipping
Edward arranged for the issue of a fresh coinage, including round halfpence and farthings, and also groats, or
*gros Tournois*, of the value of fourpence. The issue of the
smaller denominations did not please everybody, as the
beggars and the priests found that the farthing, like the
threepenny bit of modern times, supplanted the larger
coin in alms and the offertory. With the exception, however, of these two classes and the third class, those who
had made a practice and a profit of clipping coins, most
persons must have welcomed the reform of the coinage,
although the recall of the old currency caused a certain
amount of loss and inconvenience.

Early in 1279 the king spent some weeks at his favourite
Oxfordshire manor of Woodstock and from there on
12 March he issued orders for an enquiry throughout
England as to the titles by which the nobles held their
tenurial and judicial privileges and liberties. The excuse,
or rather the necessity for such an enquiry had been
afforded by the revelations of the usurpation and abuse
of privileges, to the detriment of the Crown and the
commonwealth, shown by the previous enquiry of 1274,
of which the returns had been embodied in the Hundred

Rolls. A step had been taken in the summer of 1278 by empowering the Justices in Eyre to deal with these writs of *quo warranto*—so called from their purpose being to ascertain by what warrant the privileged persons claimed their franchises. The issue of the writs and the despatch of justices to conduct the enquiry aroused the anger and consternation of the nobles, who feared the loss of many of the valuable privileges which they or their immediate predecessors had usurped from the Crown during the dotage of Henry III or at earlier periods when the royal power was feeble. A little incident showed pretty clearly the feelings of those affected. During one of his councils, possibly the identical council which issued the writs of *quo warranto*, Edward noticed the young nobles of the household talking together and evidently much amused at something; when the council was over he asked them what it was of which they were talking, and, after exacting the king's promise not to take offence, one of them repeated the epigram which had amused them.

"Le Roy coveit nos deneres
E la Reyne nos beaus maners;
E le Quo Warranto
Maketh us alle to do."

There was also a tale current at the time that when the enquiry was begun and John de Warenne, Earl of Surrey, was called upon to show his title to the almost royal franchise which he exercised in Surrey and Sussex he replied by displaying a rusty sword and saying: "See, my lords, here is my warrant. For my predecessors that came with William the Bastard conquered their lands with the sword, and with the sword I will defend them against whoever would seize them." As the earl's lands had come to him through the heiress of the Conquest de Warenne a distaff might have been a more suitable exhibit; and in any case there was no threat to his lands but only to his franchises. Whether the picturesque incident occurred or not, it is certain that it did not have the traditional effect of making King Edward abandon the enquiry, for the records show that the Earl of Surrey and all the great landowners duly appeared before the justices and allowed their claims to be examined. It is, however, possible that the opposition made and the feeling aroused caused Edward to modify his original intentions and to refrain from any sweeping resumptions of franchises. But if the enquiry involved a relatively slight curtailment of the nobles' powers, it was a wholesome reminder that they derived those powers from the Crown and could be called to account if they abused them, while the money obtained for charters of renewal and confirmation granted to those whose titles were doubtful or insecure made a useful addition to the royal revenue.

At the beginning of May 1279 Edward left Westminster for Dover, whence he crossed to France, proceeding to Amiens. Here he was met by King Philip, and on 23 May the treaty formerly made between their respective fathers, Henry III and St. Louis, was ratified. By this treaty the Agénais was made over to Edward; the three cities of Limoges, Cahors, and Perigord, however were reserved as being inalienable from the French crown, and Edward had also to surrender his claims in Aquitaine in order to obtain the cancellation of a clause inserted in the original treaty binding the French vassals of the English king to assist the French king in the event of war between the two countries. At the same time Edward obtained seisin of the two counties of Ponthieu and Aumâle, which had fallen to his wife Queen Eleanor by the death of her mother, who was the daughter of Simon de Dammartin, Count of Aumâle, and of Marie, Countess of Ponthieu.

At Amiens Edward was visited by the new Archbishop of Canterbury, John Pecham, on his way from the Roman court to England. Somewhat to the primate's surprise, and much to his relief, the king was very friendly and even assured him that he was more pleased at his appointment than he would have been if his own candidate Burnel had been accepted. As a further mark of his goodwill he at once ordered the restoration of the temporalities of the see of Canterbury to the archbishop, although by a technical error of the papal scribe formal application had not been made for them. When Pecham reached England he found this last boon to be of a shadowy nature, as the royal officers, in whose hands the estates of the see had been during the vacancy, had stripped the manors bare; moreover, owing to the judicial proceedings relative to clipped money and the fact that a new coinage was shortly to be issued there was practically no money in circulation in England, and it was also a year of great dearth. The unfortunate archbishop had borrowed 4,000 marks from the merchants of Lucca, one of the chief banking firms of this period, for his expenses at the papal court and would incur sentence of excommunication if he failed to pay. To complicate matters, he found that the merchants of Lucca were under the influence of "a certain bishop", whom we may identify as Burnel the Chancellor, whose evil life he wished to expose and punish. Undeterred by all these misfortunes the energetic primate, immediately after he landed in England, issued orders for a provincial synod to meet at Reading on 30 July, and also endeavoured to suspend the proceedings of the justices in *quo warranto* against the Earl of Gloucester, on the ground that the rights of the see of Canterbury were involved. Later in the year he displayed vigour, and even violence, in carrying on the traditional quarrel with the rival see of York, his servants forcibly depriving the northern primate of the cross which he attempted to have carried before him in derogation of Canterbury's dignity.

Edward returned from France on 17 June, after a month's absence, and shortly afterwards wrote to Alphonso of Castile, who had become alarmed at the improvement in the relations between England and

France, reassuring him. As a mark of his friendship he sent him some grey gerfalcons, apologising for not sending any white ones as he had recently lost nine and had none left; he added that he had sent to Norway for some more and hoped soon to bring them himself. Relations with Norway were very cordial at this time; presents were frequently exchanged between the two kings, as for instance in 1276 when King Magnus sent to King Edward three white gerfalcons and eight grey, a quantity of ermine skins and "the whole head of a whale, with the teeth, in the hope that it might interest the king's excellency and redound to the glory of the marvellous Creator". He added that if asked the bearer of the present would explain the wonderful nature of the beast, which, we may be sure, lost nothing in the telling. On the other hand, in September 1279 King Edward sent to Magnus certain relics for which he had asked. The gift was acknowledged in May 1280 by Magnus, who wrote from his death-bed commending to Edward's good graces his successor Eric and his younger son Hacon and sending a further present of gentle falcons.

While foreign affairs were going thus smoothly Edward was experiencing a certain amount of friction at home. The attack upon the privileges of the nobles had led to wild rumours that no man would be allowed to reap his own corn or mow his own meadow and the king was obliged to take steps against the spreaders of these rumours. The clergy also were giving trouble; at the synod held at Reading on 30 July 1279 Archbishop Pecham took up a strong line against the holders of pluralities, which included most of the royal clerks, and ordered the excommunication of all who interfered with the liberty and jurisdiction of the Church and ecclesiastical courts, further directing that the portions of Magna Carta dealing with the liberty of the Church should be affixed to the doors of cathedrals and collegiate churches. Edward made no immediate move and was even present at Canterbury on 8 October when Pecham was formally installed; but if the archbishop shared the general belief of his age in portents he might have drawn an omen from the great snow-storm which swept over England on the day after his installation. At the parliament held at Westminster Pecham was obliged to withdraw the greater part of the sentences promulgated at Reading so far as they related to the clashing of the civil and ecclesiastical courts, and also to remove the copies of Magna Carta from the church doors. More serious was Edward's counterblow in the Statute *De Religiosis*, the first Act of Mortmain, by which the alienation of estates to religious corporations was entirely forbidden. With this came a demand for a subsidy from the clergy. In summoning a Convocation to consider this demand Pecham pointed out to his suffragans the need to obtain the royal favour and the dangers which recent experiences had shown might result from the failure to do so; he further argued that as the laity had granted an aid to the king it was not for the clergy to be behind them in generosity and he urged that the king should not be angered by too small a grant. Following the lead thus given them the clergy of Canterbury agreed to a fifteenth for three years, the clergy of the northern province making the equivalent grant of a tenth for two years.

Neither Edward nor Pecham would lightly abandon his position and the conflict between Church and State continued for some time, though without any actual breach. In the spring of 1280 the archbishop insisted on holding a visitation of the royal chapels and in reply to the king's prohibition, on the ground of their being exempt, expressed his desire to uphold the royal rights in every way short of mortal sin but warned the king that he must be prepared to take the responsibility for the sins of his chaplains if he refused to allow the Church to correct them. In the matter of pluralities also Pecham acted with determination, refusing to consecrate to the see of Winchester the pluralist Richard de la More, who had been elected after the Pope had quashed the election of the Chancellor Burnel. But in view of the prevalence of pluralities in England and the impossibility of reducing the wealthy clergy to sudden poverty he pointed out to Pope Nicholas III the need for exercising moderation in dealing with this question. He was also unable to obtain the king's consent to the requests made in 1280 by this Pope and by his successor Martin IV for the release of Aumary de Montfort, who was eventually restored to liberty in April 1282. Twice when Pecham summoned synods, in January 1280 and October 1281, to deal with the respective jurisdictions of the church and lay courts Edward intervened with a stern warning that nothing should be done to affect his prerogative. On both occasions Pecham gave way, but in November 1281 he wrote a long letter to the king urging him to submit to the authority of the Pope, advancing many arguments and quoting many precedents. This no doubt relieved the archbishop's feelings. At the same time Pecham adhered to his policy of keeping on good terms with Edward so far as conscience allowed, and he even incurred the anger of his subordinate clergy by making no stand against the proposals for their taxation when money was required for the Welsh campaigns. The archbishop, indeed, worked strenuously on the king's behalf throughout the troubled times which, beginning in 1281, ended in the final overthrow of the principality of Wales and its union with England in 1283.

Seal of Edward I

Denbigh Castle

Harlech Castle

# Chapter Four

# Welsh Affairs

In order to treat the Welsh war of 1282–83 satisfactorily, alike from the political and military point of view, it is necessary to consider it in conjunction with the earlier campaign of 1277. In the first place it must be borne in mind that before the extinction of its independence Wales was a geographical expression rather than a nation. At the end of the thirteenth century the North Welsh and the South Welsh were still as distinct from one another as they had been a century earlier when Gerald de Barri wrote his description of Wales and, as at that earlier date, the men of the North still clung to their traditional weapon the long spear while the men of the South had continued and developed the use of the bow, a fact of considerable military significance. The Welsh had no acknowledged supreme chief with even the shadowy supremacy of the Saxon Bretwalda or Irish Ard-Righ, but in the course of time the princes of Gwynedd, or North Wales, had been tacitly accepted as the national leaders and even accorded the title of Princes of Wales. This was due partly to the great natural strength of their fastnesses in the wooded mountains of Snowdon, partly to their control of the grain-lands of Anglesey, but mainly to the personalities of Llewelyn the Great and of his grandson Llewelyn ap Gruffudd. The latter prince, as we have seen, had successfully defied Edward before his accession, had been the valued ally of Simon de Montfort when he staggered the royal

E

power of England and had escaped from the ruin that
fell upon Montfort's party with an impunity implying
a recognition of his strength. Had Llewelyn been content
to accept the light yoke of the shadowy English suzerainty it is conceivable that he might have preserved his
substantial independence, though it must be admitted
that he would probably sooner or later have been drawn
into conflict with Edward through inevitable quarrels
with his neighbours such as Gruffudd ap Gwenwynwyn
of Powys or the marcher lords. However, he evaded or
ignored, with varying degrees of insolence, all demands
for the performance of homage and unwisely persisted
in marrying Simon de Montfort's daughter Eleanor, with
the hope, no doubt, of forming a party against the king.
But Montfort was no longer a name to conjure with,
the bride fell into Edward's hands, and no English baron
would move a finger to help either her or the Welsh
prince. Finally Edward's patience was exhausted and in
November 1276 Llewelyn was pronounced contumacious
and rebellious and preparations were made for war. For
a time Edward contented himself with operations on a
small scale; the Earl of Warwick was put in command of
a force at Chester, Roger de Mortimer at Montgomery,
and Payn de Chaworth at Carmarthen, and in January
1277 a considerable reinforcement was sent under the
Earl of Lincoln. These leaders, with local levies from the
western counties, rapidly recovered the marches of
Cheshire and Shropshire, into which Llewelyn had
penetrated, and occupied Powys on behalf of Gruffudd
ap Gwenwynwyn. Then in the centre Mortimer recovered
his castles of Dolforwyn and Builth, or at least as much
of them as the Welsh had left standing, and the districts
which they commanded, while further south Chaworth
reduced Rhys ap Maredudd of Dynevor, Prince of South
Wales, a half-hearted ally of Llewelyn, to terms. Meanwhile Edward was making elaborate preparations for the
main campaign, the opening of which had been fixed for

July 1277. Provisions and munitions were being accumulated, remounts were being purchased in France, though King Philip put difficulties in the way of their being sent over to England, and a small contingent of Gascon mercenaries, mostly mounted crossbowmen, equivalent to the mounted infantry of more recent times, were engaged. In addition to the actual fighting men a large number of miners, carpenters and masons impressed from all parts of England, constituted a corps of engineers and a small fleet under the command of the Warden of the Cinque Ports, Stephen de Pencestre, was to cooperate with the land forces.

After mustering at Worcester at the beginning of July the army moved up to Chester and then to new headquarters at a protected camp near Basingwerk. Knowing the danger of advancing into the densely wooded country which lay in front of him, Edward sent his engineers and woodmen forward, under an escort of crossbowmen and archers, to clear a broad road through the forest. Thus secured from ambushes and with his right flank and communications covered by the fleet, Edward was able to advance to Rhuddlan at the end of August and after a brief halt reached Diganwy at the mouth of the River Conway on 1 September. The Welsh appear to have selected the strategically excellent position on the left bank of the Conway estuary to oppose the English advance, but Edward sent a strong force over to Anglesey, thereby threatening Llewelyn's rear and at the same time securing for his own use the harvest of the island, on which the Welsh were almost entirely dependent for their corn crops. Meanwhile an army under the king's brother, Edmund of Lancaster, had been operating in South Wales and after meeting with little opposition had advanced as far as Aberystwyth, where preparations had at once been made for the building of a great castle. Alarmed at the steady onward sweep of the English armies and unencouraged by any successful forays,

Llewelyn, whose Welsh temperament was liable to fits of pessimism, abandoned the struggle and made an appeal for peace to which Edward gladly responded.

By the treaty signed at Rhuddlan on 9 November 1277 the Four Cantreds, in the north-east corner of Wales, were surrendered by Llewelyn and two of them, including the fortresses of Hope and Denbigh, were at once made over to his brother David, Edward's ally during the campaign. The English frontier was thus thrust forward to the River Conway, and to secure control of the coast road a new castle was begun at Rhuddlan and a second at Flint. In the centre of Wales, Mortimer's destroyed castle at Builth was reconstructed on a much larger scale as a royal fortress, while Mortimer himself was licensed to rebuild Cefnllys and took the opportunity to enlarge and strengthen it to a degree which alarmed Llewelyn into a useless protest. On the west coast the castle begun at Aberystwyth was completed and the town itself surrounded with a wall, while at Montgomery the stockade which had formerly protected the town was replaced by masonry. The marcher lords, we may be sure, followed the example of their royal master in strengthening their holds, but the operation which gave most annoyance to the Welsh and promised most security for the future was the thinning of the forests and the cutting of broad roadways through the woods.

In addition to these strictly military precautions Edward took certain political measures for the pacification of the country, including the introduction of the shire system, with county courts and other features of English jurisdiction. That it was the king's intention to govern the parts of Wales that were now under his control with justice and gain the goodwill of the inhabitants cannot be doubted. There is also reason to believe that he was in some considerable measure successful so far as the common people were concerned, but the chieftains and petty lords were too long accustomed to that form of licence which they called liberty to accept the restraints of English law even if administered with strict impartiality, and from what we know of contemporary English officials in their own country we may feel fairly sure that cases of maladministration and oppression were not lacking. Llewelyn himself complained that each successive official was harsher than his predecessor; he protested that the Sheriff of Shropshire favoured his rival and enemy Gruffudd of Powys unduly; he resented being summoned to attend the court at Montgomery and still more being forbidden to build a castle in his own territory. It was, however, not Llewelyn but his brother David who at last kindled the flame of rebellion in Wales. David had originally been driven out of Wales by his brother and had sought refuge at the English court, where he had been more than kindly received by Edward. Having fought against Llewelyn in 1277 he had been rewarded with a substantial grant of lands in the neighbourhood of Denbigh and Edward had also bestowed upon him the hand of Elizabeth Ferrers, daughter of the former Earl of Derby. He had not, however, obtained as great a territory as he had hoped and, so far from supplanting Llewelyn as Prince of Gwynedd, he was definitely excluded from all hopes of succeeding to the princedom by the Treaty of Rhuddlan, while his subordinate position was emphasised by his being summoned before the Justiciar of Chester to prove his title to certain estates. Suddenly, without warning, on 21 March 1282 David swept down in the darkness of the night upon Hawarden Castle, overpowered the garrison and carried off the constable, Roger de Clifford. In an instant all North Wales rose. Attempts to seize the castles of Rhuddlan and Flint were unsuccessful but Ruthin and Dinas Bran fell into the hands of the Welsh and in the south Llandovery and the castle-crowned crag of Caercynan were captured by Rhys ap Maelgwyn and Gruffudd ap Maredudd. Still more important was the seizure and destruction of the new great castle at Aberystwyth by Gruffudd and Llewelyn ap Rhys Vychan. Alone of the Welsh chieftains (for Gruffudd ap Gwenwynwyn was so identified with English interests that he was practically a marcher lord) Rhys ap Maredudd remained loyal to Edward.

News of the rising reached Edward at Devizes on 25 March. He promptly sent orders to Reynold de Grey to take command at Chester and Roger de Mortimer at Montgomery, with the support of levies from the adjacent counties; in South Wales Robert de Tibotot was in command and the Earls of Hereford and Gloucester were associated with him, Gloucester being afterwards given the nominal command. Orders were also sent to the merchants and trading guilds of London to arrange for a war loan, and a council was summoned to meet at Devizes. Informal summonses or "requests" were sent out for the assembling of forces at Worcester on 17 May. Before that date had arrived troops had been collected on all the marches sufficient to hold the Welsh fairly well in check but not to make any substantial progress in suppressing the rebellion. On his arrival at Worcester Edward found that the gentry had answered loyally to his requests and that a good number of fighting men had been collected. He then issued writs to all his feudal tenants to be at Rhuddlan on 2 August to perform their due military service of forty days. Meanwhile he himself pushed on to Chester, reaching that city on 6 June. Grey's forces had not been idle; the district between Chester and Rhuddlan had been cleared and the town of St. Asaph, which the enemy had tried to hold, had been burnt, involving the destruction of the cathedral; the Welsh, with a wise distrust of castles, do not seem to have held Hawarden and had dismantled and abandoned Hope before the middle of the month. In the south affairs had not gone well. Inspired by the presence of Llewelyn, the Welsh had prevented Gloucester from re-establishing himself at either Aberystwyth or Llandovery and had compelled him to remain practically on the defensive. On 17 June, when returning from Dynevor to Caercynan, where arrangements were being made for rebuilding the castle, the English were surprised and badly cut up at Llandeilo Fawr. Gloucester at once abandoned Carmarthenshire and was superseded by the Earl of Pembroke, whose son William de Valence had fallen at Llandeilo.

In the north David had made Denbigh his base and the English were operating against him from Rhuddlan, which the king had reached on 8 July, and from Hope, where Grey was in command. As in 1277, the king had the support of a fleet and on 18 August, after the musters were completed, he sent a strong force under Luke de Tany, formerly Seneschal of Gascony, to occupy Anglesey. Besides seizing the grain crops of the island Tany was charged with the construction of a bridge of boats to the mainland in order to take the Welsh in the rear when Edward advanced to the Conway. This bridge was built under the protection of the ships of the Cinque Ports and was practically completed by the end of September 1282, but orders were given that no attack should be made across it until the king gave the command. The general advance now began. Grey had advanced to Ruthin and had been joined there by the king, who in the middle of September transferred his headquarters to Llangerniew, west of Denbigh, which town, thus ringed in, fell in October and became Edward's headquarters. The fall of Denbigh compelled David to retire to Snowdon and Llewelyn hastened to his assistance. The position was now very similar to that in 1277 when Llewelyn had come to terms, and accordingly Archbishop Pecham was authorised to negotiate with the Welsh prince. To his endeavour to put the whole blame on the Welsh, Llewelyn replied by presenting a list of grievances which he alleged justified his action. Edward's reply that the rebellion was inexcusable because Llewelyn had not laid

these complaints before him and that he would always
have done him justice if he had done so would be more
convincing if there were not still extant a large number
of letters written by Llewelyn to Edward before the war
complaining of many of the grievances now advanced.
The terms which Pecham offered, including Llewelyn's
retirement to England on a pension and David's banishment on a pilgrimage to the Holy Land, could only have
been acceptable if the Welsh princes had been in desperate
straits. Their position, as a matter of fact, appeared far
from desperate; in the south the English were barely
holding their own and in the north their advance had
been slow and had not yet penetrated into the moun-
tainous district of Snowdon. Moreover they seem to have
suffered a setback during the advance from Hope Castle,
and while the negotiations were actually in progress the
forces garrisoning Anglesey were involved in a disaster
which must have given great encouragement to the
Welsh. In spite of strict orders to the contrary Luke de
Tany on 6 November crossed the bridge of boats with
some hundred and fifty lances, either for purposes of
reconnaissance or of plunder. On the mainland they were
surprised by the Welsh in unexpected numbers and,
seized with sudden panic, galloped for the head of the
bridge. Owing to the rise of the tide access to the bridge
was difficult and in the confused struggle for safety
almost all the raiders, encumbered by their armour, were
drowned or slaughtered, including Tany himself and
most of his bannerets.

The negotiations for peace were at once broken off,
Edward fell back on his bases and remained on the
defensive while he made preparation for a winter
campaign. Satisfied with the position in the north,
Llewelyn dashed southwards to raid the Hereford march
and the district round Builth. Close to this latter castle
his forces took up their position on the hills, protected
from the English under John Giffard by the River Yrfon

and commanding Orewin Bridge. On 11 December a Welshman showed the English a ford, by which a body of cavalry crossed and, attacking the Welsh in the rear, seized Orewin Bridge and enabled the whole of Giffard's forces to cross. Finding themselves surrounded, the Welsh formed up in a solid mass ringed round with a bristling hedge of spears. Such a formation, excellent for defence against unsupported cavalry, has no offensive value and when Giffard brought up his bowmen, skilfully mingling them with the cavalry, the fate of the Welsh was sealed. Lacking defensive armour they fell rapidly before the storm of missiles, to which, owing to their lack of archers, they could make no effective reply and as the gaps in their ranks grew the English lances charged in and completed the rout. Llewelyn himself was not present when the battle began but hearing news of it he hastened back to rejoin his men; on the way he encountered a body of English and in the fight that followed he was slain, unrecognised, by one Stephen de Frankton. Not until the bodies were being despoiled was it discovered that the famous chieftain had fallen. Llewelyn's absence from his forces at the critical moment has been attributed by some authorities to his having been lured away by a message from the Mortimers pretending to be willing to assist him against Edward, and this is borne out by Archbishop Pecham's allusion to a letter found on Llewelyn's body which appeared to involve some of the marcher lords in a charge of treason.

The head of the fallen prince was brought to King Edward and by him sent first to be displayed to the army in Anglesey and then to London, where on 22 December the citizens carried it, crowned in mockery with ivy, through the streets with a triumphant noise of horns and trumpets, to be set up first upon the pillory and then on the battlements of the Tower. While the death of Llewelyn removed Edward's most able opponent it by no means ended the war. South Wales, it is true, had been quieted by the end of 1282 but in Gwynedd David was maintaining the struggle. Meanwhile Edward's forces were growing; during January 1283 fresh levies were continually coming in and the armies, both in Anglesey and Rhuddlan, had been much strengthened by troops of Gascon mercenaries. From Bordeaux came 400 crossbowmen under Guichard de Bourg; Gaston de Béarn sent 15 knights and 300 unmounted crossbowmen; the Vicomte de Tarcazin led in person a similar force; while other formidable troops were led by Roger de Mauleon, Arnald de Gaveston, the Counts of Armagnac and Bigorre, and John de Vescy. In the middle of January Edward struck southwards, making his headquarters at Llanwrts and Bettws-y-Coed on the Conway and thence attacking Dolwyddelan Castle, which was speedily reduced. Having garrisoned this stronghold in the centre of the Snowdon district as a base for future operations, the king withdrew to Rhuddlan and allowed the bulk of his English levies to return home. On 13 March Edward transferred his army to the mouth of the Conway, where he remained for two months arranging for the erection of the noble castle of Conway, which was begun this year. The war had dwindled to a hunt for David with little more than isolated skirmishes to vary the monotony, except for a brief flare up at the end of March when David, abandoning Snowdon, managed to establish a force in Bere Castle, near Cader Idris. Bere was soon reduced, David fled north again and Edward hunted him remorselessly. At last, at the end of June 1283, the fugitive prince with his family was caught by some of his own countrymen and handed over to the English. On 30 September a parliament met at Shrewsbury to try him for treason and on 2 October he suffered the doom of a traitor, being drawn, hanged, and quartered. The Mayor of London and his five associates, who had represented the City at the trial, carried back with them David's head, to be set beside that of his brother on the heights of the Tower, while the quarters of his body were sent to Winchester, Northampton, Chester and York; his sons were imprisoned at Bristol and his daughters were immured in nunneries, sharing the fate of Llewelyn's infant daughter, whose mother Eleanor de Montfort had died in giving birth to her in June 1282.

After the execution of David, Welsh resistance was at an end and it only remained to establish the English rule firmly throughout the principality and to take precautions against future risings. During the latter half of 1283 castles were being built at Conway and Carnarvon, the latter being sufficiently advanced by 25 April 1284 to shelter Queen Eleanor when she gave birth to a son, Edward "of Carnarvon", thus enabling the king to put the principality of Wales into the hands of a prince who could at least claim the allegiance of his subjects as being Welsh-born. The older castles of Dolwyddelan, Criccieth, Harlech, Bere, and Aberystwyth were repaired and greatly strengthened. In addition to these physical measures for controlling the natives the Statute of Wales, passed on 19 March 1284, introduced the shire system into those parts where it did not yet prevail and, for all practical purposes, brought Wales under the same legal system as existed in England. About the end of 1283, when writing to press for the payment of the subsidy voted by the clergy, Edward was able to say that at last the snake in the grass which had so long troubled England was scotched and the poison purged from the wound in England's side; but for the first nine months of 1284 he remained almost continuously either actually in North Wales or on the marches, and in September he began a progress through the principality. Archbishop Pecham, consciously or unconsciously reproducing the advice of Gerald de Barri a century earlier, had suggested that the Welsh should be tamed by compelling them to live in towns, and it was doubtless to encourage this practice, and also to attract English settlers, that Edward bestowed the privileges of free boroughs upon Flint, Rhuddlan, Conway, Carnarvon, Criccieth, Harlech and Bere, making the constable of the castle in each case mayor. The king reached Aberystwyth on 8 November and Cardigan ten days later; he then turned eastwards by Carmarthen and Kidwelly to Glamorgan, where he was received by the Earl of Gloucester with a somewhat ostentatious display of courtesy which emphasised the power of a marcher lord in his own district but did not render it more acceptable to King Edward.

On 20 December Edward crossed the Severn to Bristol, where he kept Christmas 1284, and when he left England eighteen months later on his long visit to Gascony he can have felt little anxiety about affairs in Wales. By the end of 1286, however, Rhys ap Meredudd, who had been his staunch ally so long as the princes of Gwynedd had been the leaders of rebellion, was showing signs of restiveness. The loss of Dynevor, the ancestral seat of his line, which Edward had retained in his own hands, the control exercised by Tibotot as Justiciar of West Wales, and the irritating restrictions incidental to the introduction of English law, coupled no doubt with grievances of a more definite nature, at last exasperated Rhys into active revolt. In June 1287 he seized Dynevor, Caercynan, and Llandovery castles and made a series of raids from Carmarthen to Swansea and even as far north as Aberystwyth. The absence of the king may have encouraged his hopes, but the Earl of Cornwall as regent acted with vigour and promptitude. In a remarkably short time very large forces from all the marches were concentrating on the valley of the Towey; by the middle of August the captured castles had been retaken and early in September Rhy's own castle of Drysylwyn was reduced. Although Rhys was still at large the rebellion seemed to be crushed and the regent withdrew his troops; but in November Rhys suddenly seized the castle of Emlyn and it was not retaken until the middle of January 1288, after which time

Rhys gave no more trouble, though it was not until April 1291 that he was caught and executed. With the downfall of Rhys ap Meredudd the line of the princes of South Wales came to an end, as that of the princes of Gwynedd had already done, and except for the rising of 1294–95, to which reference will be made later, the Welsh gave no more trouble during Edward's reign.

# Chapter Five

# High Noon

The eight years that followed his conquest of the
principality of Wales may be said to mark the zenith of
Edward's reign. His relations with all the continental
powers were good, or at least satisfactory, his position as
a ruler was so well recognised that he was in constant
demand as arbiter or mediator between his contemporaries,
while his acknowledged pre-eminence as a crusader compelled the successive occupants of the papal throne to
connive at much in his policy that was distinctly anti-
clerical. During those eight years the last smouldering
embers of Welsh independence were quenched, the
unruly Gascons were brought to order, his continental
position was strengthened by matrimonial alliances and
at home the successful assertion of his right to the overlordship of Scotland gave promise, delusive indeed, of
peace and security. The succession to the English throne
was also rendered more secure by the birth, at Carnarvon
on 25 April 1284, of another royal prince, called after his
father, Edward. Unfortunately, just four months later,
his elder brother Alphonso, then in his twelfth year,
died, to the great grief of his parents. Of Alphonso we
know but little; we may read of purchases of toys, a cart,
a gaily painted cross-bow or a wooden model of a castle,
of clothes or chaplets of flowers for him, or in later years
of hawks and hounds. In the early summer of 1284 he
offered a golden torque which had belonged to Llewelyn
and other jewels at Westminster for the adornment of the

shrine of St. Edward, close to which he was buried a few months later, and only a few days before his death negotiations for his marriage to a daughter of Florence, Count of Holland, had been concluded, but of the boy himself we know nothing. It is true that contemporary chroniclers speak of him in terms of high praise—*Flos juvenum, spes militum, patrisque solamen* and so forth—but they would have applied the same terms to his brother Edward had good fortune decreed that he should die in early youth.

The death of the young Prince Alphonso occurred, as chance would have it, within a year after the death of the godfather whose name he bore, his uncle Alphonso X of Castile. Edward had always been on good terms with his brother-in-law and had on more than one occasion endeavoured to compose the quarrel between him and Philip of France; he had gladly evaded the demand of his feudal overlord, Philip, for assistance against Alphonso on the ground of the troubled state of Welsh affairs, and had been largely instrumental in procuring peace between the two kings in 1280, though he had been unable to be present in person at Bayonne on the occasion of their meeting. It was indeed Edward's constant aim to avoid war whenever possible and to compose the quarrels of his neighbours so far as it was in his power to do so. During the one year 1284 we find him acting as arbiter between the Duke of Brabant and the Count of Guelders and also between the same Duke and the Count of Holland, renewing and confirming his friendship with Eric of Norway, and, in conjunction with his mother Eleanor, settling the question of the succession to the county of Savoy. He also played a considerable part in the affairs of Pedro III of Aragon. Pedro, in right of his wife Constance, daughter of Manfred, laid claim to the throne of Sicily against Charles of Anjou, who had ousted Manfred some twenty years earlier. On Easter Monday, 30 March 1282, the Sicilians rose and massacred the whole French population of Palermo and Messina; in August of the same year Pedro landed at Trapani and on 2 October the Aragonese fleet gained a decisive victory over the French. The Pope, by the authority of whose predecessors Charles had been installed in Sicily, hurled excommunication and empty decrees of deposition against Pedro, who had meanwhile come to an agreement with his adversary that their dispute should be settled by a duel of one hundred knights on each side; King Edward, as the foremost patron of tournaments and chivalry, was asked to allow the duel to be fought at Bordeaux and to preside in person or by deputy. The application of the principles of chivalry to a dispute of this importance is unique, and the idea that a quarrel over a throne should be settled by a single combat between the actual disputants rather than by the traditional method of slaughtering and despoiling their unfortunate subjects horrifies even that cautious historian Sir James Ramsay into the use of the unusually full-blooded adjective "preposterous". Sir James's further statement that it was condemned by "Edward's good sense" is misleading. What Edward condemned was war in any form between the two kings; by allowing them to fight in his territory and acting as judge he would be encouraging the violent settlement of a dispute which it was his desire to compose without bloodshed. His good sense showed him that he might be placed in a very awkward position by having to give a decision against either party and he had written from Conway on 25 March 1283 refusing to countenance the duel, some few days before Pope Martin wrote urging him to use his influence to prevent it. Of the disputants, Charles was Edward's cousin and had always been on good terms with him, while Edward was at the time negotiating for the marriage of his eldest daughter Eleanor with Alphonso, eldest son of Pedro. This last project was regarded with disfavour by Pope Martin, nominally on the ground that the parties were related in

Queen Margaret

Seal of John Baliol

Seal of Robert Bruce

the fourth degree, a convenient excuse for quashing inconvenient alliances between most of the reigning families of the Continent.

Edward had left Wales shortly before Christmas 1284, which feast he spent at Bristol. While there he held a special parliament, probably to decide what action should be taken in regard to the summons sent him by King Philip III for assistance against Pedro of Aragon. It would seem that he decided to obey the summons in person but with the object rather of mediating than of giving armed assistance to his overlord, for although he made his way to Dover at the end of January 1285 there is no evidence of any military force having been levied to accompany him. While at Dover he received the satisfactory news that a truce had been made between France and Aragon and he at once turned back and, after spending two months in the eastern counties, visiting Bury St. Edmund's and Ely, re-entered London at the end of April. Three years had passed since he had visited the capital and he was accordingly received with much magnificence and rejoicing. His first act was to go in solemn procession from the Tower to Westminster Abbey, of which the rebuilding initiated by his father had just been brought to a conclusion, preceded by Archbishop Pecham carrying the holy cross of St. Neot. Having offered upon the high altar this symbol of his conquest of Wales he returned to his palace to open a parliament, which sat for seven weeks and on 28 June published the lengthy codification of laws relating to landed property known as the Second Statute of Westminster. It was at this time Edward's intention to cross over to France and as early as 4 June he had appointed Aymer de Valence, Earl of Pembroke, guardian of the realm in his absence. In July he moved down towards Dover and spent some two weeks in the neighbourhood of Canterbury and Leeds, but King Philip was now fighting in Spain and Edward, hearing that his mother

F

Queen Eleanor was lying ill at Amesbury, abandoned his projected tour and turned west. The Queen Mother, who possessed much of her late husband's inconsiderate piety, had long since persuaded her son reluctantly to promise that his daughter Mary should become a nun of the order of Fontevrault. This promise was now fulfilled, the princess being received into the priory of Amesbury, a cell of Fontevrault, on 15 August 1285, with fourteen other girls of noble birth, to the grief of her parents. Mary's own feelings on the subject can hardly have been decided as she was only in her seventh year. Nearly a year later, on 7 July 1286, the old Queen Eleanor herself took the veil at Amesbury, modifying the vow of poverty by retaining her very substantial dowry under a special papal dispensation.

From Amesbury Edward went to Clarendon and later to Winchester, where he bestowed the honour of knighthood on some forty or fifty young nobles and held a parliament which issued, on 8 October, the Statute of Winchester, a reaffirmation of existing regulations for the policing of the country, which had been allowed to lapse with the result that crimes of violence had become alarmingly prevalent. Leaving Winchester in the middle of October the king spent a couple of weeks in the Isle of Wight. While there he received news of the death of Philip III, which had occurred shortly after that of his adversary Pedro III of Aragon. Pedro's other chief adversaries Charles of Anjou and Pope Martin IV had also died during this same year 1285, and on 18 March 1286 there followed the death of Alexander III of Scotland, fraught with evil for England in later years. About the same time also died William Wikwane, Archbishop of York, and Hugh, Bishop of Ely, to whose see was elected John de Kirkby, Edward's unpopular Treasurer,—

*Non est inventus similis tibi Kirkebyensis,*
*Nemine contentus, labiis ad jurgia tensis.*

At last, on 13 May 1286, Edward started on his long deferred journey to France, crossing from Dover to Wissant. At Amiens the royal visitors were met by the young King Philip IV, "le Bel", who escorted them to Paris, where they spent June and July. On 5 June Edward did homage to Philip for the estates which he ought to hold of him, on the understanding that those cessions still due under the treaty of 1259 should be completed, these claims being eventually settled by the cession of Saintonge south of Charente and a rent of 3,000 *livres Tournois*, equivalent to £750 of English money, Philip at the same time making liberal concessions with regard to appeals made to his court from the courts of Gascony. Edward was also busy negotiating a truce between his royal host and Alphonso of Aragon and endeavouring to obtain the consent of Pope Honorius IV to the terms suggested. During his stay in Paris the king had a remarkable escape from sudden death, when lightning passed through a window in front of which he and Queen Eleanor were sitting, and killed two of their attendants. In addition to his diplomatic business with France and Aragon Edward had much to occupy his attention in Gascony, an unrestful district full of minor lordships whose rulers were perpetually at daggers drawn with their neighbours. The king, therefore, left Paris early in August and travelled slowly down through Pontigny and Orleans to undertake a comprehensive visitation of his French dominions. Christmas was spent in the little town of St. Macaire, near Bordeaux, the court being lodged in the priory, of which the church was used as the king's hall. Here the festival was observed in the usual manner, with the exchange of gifts—the once rebellious Gaston de Béarn gave chargers to both king and queen, the lord of Mirabeau two hawks, Anthony Bek, the king's faithful clerk promoted to the see of Durham in 1283, a sporting hound, and Edmund of Lancaster a quantity of the cheese for which Brie was already famous. Nor was music lacking, in quantity, whatever its quality may have been, for no fewer than 125 minstrels benefited by the royal largesse. Early in January 1287 the court removed to Bordeaux and about the end of March we find Edward hunting wolves and stopping for a meal at the house of a man with the romantic name of Dawe de les Laundes. But shortly afterwards the king was taken seriously ill at Blanquefort; fortunately the skill of Philip de Beauvais and his other physicians speedily restored him to health. It was probably as a thank offering for his recovery that he made the lavish gift of £100 to the rector of St. Mary, Uzeste, for the rebuilding of his chancel, and it was certainly for this reason that he went to Bordeaux and with a great number of followers took the cross from the papal legate and was appointed by him leader of the Christian army for the next crusade.

Ever since his accession Edward had been playing with the idea of going again to the Holy Land; how far he was in earnest it would be difficult to say. He was recognised as "the prince of Christendom who has the Holy Land most at heart and knows it best" and appeals for help were constantly being made to him by the popes, the members of the military orders still maintaining a desperate grip on the outer fringe of Palestine, and by the Tartars and other opportunist Christian tribes who were striving to evict the Saracens. While he was at St. Sever in October 1287 he received "Mar de Barsauma, Bishop of the East, ambassador of Argon, Khan of the Tartars", and at the first parliament after his return to England he gave audience to another embassy from Argon, to whom he promised an army and actually sent a present of falcons and greyhounds. So far as the popes were concerned it was Edward's habitual practice to become enthusiastic over crusading propositions whenever he was in want of money and thereby to obtain grants of clerical subsidies, which he promptly applied to other purposes. It is probable that he was more in earnest than usual on this occasion, and there may have been some connection between his convalescent vow of crusade and the arrest by his orders, in May 1287, of all those enemies of the Christian faith, the Jews, in England. Their subsequent release on payment of a fine of 20,000 marks is evidence that he did not allow religion to interfere with business principles.

King Edward and Eleanor were at Bordeaux on 28 May 1287, when they observed the anniversary of the death of one of their daughters, who was buried in the church of the Friars Preachers there. Of this daughter's identity nothing is known, no historian apparently having recorded her birth or death, unless possibly she is the child who is said to have died at Acre. Meanwhile Edward's negotiations for peace between France and Aragon, which turned chiefly upon the release of Prince Charles of Salerno, son of the late King Charles of Anjou, were being brought to a conclusion. It was arranged that Alphonso of Aragon should come to Oloron, and accordingly the English court moved to that town on 17 July, finding such lodging as they best could, the monastery being put at the disposal of the Spanish. Here ten days were spent in feasting, dancing and tilting, gardens and vineyards being levelled to form an arena for the Spaniards' games and mimic battles, and here on 25 July a treaty was signed. By this treaty there was to be a truce of three years, Prince Charles was to be released at once and within the three years to obtain from the Pope and from King Philip the recognition of Alphonso as King of Aragon and of his brother Jayme as King of Sicily, or, in default, to place himself or his county of Provence in the hands of Alphonso. As guarantees Charles had to give his three eldest sons, with sixty sons of magnates of Provence, as hostages and to deposit securities to the value of 50,000 marks. To this treaty Pope Nicholas IV immediately after his election in February 1288 gave uncompromising opposition, at the same time demanding the release of Charles. At last, on 28 October 1288, a treaty was signed by Alphonso, Edward and Charles at Canfranc in Aragon, in which nothing was said about the kingdom of Sicily and the liabilities of Charles, both as to hostages and pecuniary obligations, were discharged by Edward. No sooner had Charles been released than Pope Nicholas quashed the treaty, liberated him from the conditions which he had sworn to observe and crowned him King of Sicily. To this act of treachery Edward was no party but he could take no active steps to enforce the treaty.

Immediately after his liberation Charles had returned with Edward to Oloron, where on 3 November 1288 he executed various deeds binding him to perform the obligations which he had incurred to the English king. He then went to Provence, Sir John de Vescy accompanying him to hasten the despatch of the Provençal hostages who were to take the place of those provided by Edward. Charles showed no anxiety to anticipate the term of three months allowed him and Sir John died at Montpellier on 23 February 1289 before the hostages had started. But at last the exchange was made and on 9 March the English and Gascon hostages were released, King Edward riding out towards the Spanish frontier to meet them. Meanwhile his English subjects were becoming impatient of his long stay in Aquitaine; the absence of the king had led to an increase of lawlessness; in July 1288 the great fair at Boston, one of the most important annual fixtures of the trading world, was interrupted by a sort of rough tournament between two parties of riotous young men, disguised respectively as monks and canons, who ended by joining forces under one Robert Chamberlain, sacking the fair and setting fire to the town, inflicting immense damage and loss upon the assembled merchants. Next month the regency council had to issue orders to the magnates throughout England forbidding them to ride about the country with bands of armed retainers, and in June 1289 a special mandate was addressed to the Earl of Gloucester, who was carrying on a species of private war with the Earl of Hereford on the Welsh March, ordering him to keep the peace. Moreover, in the absence of the Chancellor, the king's justices and other officials, never over-scrupulous in such matters as taking bribes, had perverted the course of justice to their own advantage. All ranks and classes were in a state of irritation and discontent and at the parliament held in the early spring of 1289 a demand for a subsidy to meet the expenses of Edward's visit to Aquitaine was met with a blunt refusal to grant any supplies until he returned to England, a refusal the more weighty from its being pronounced by Earl Gilbert of Gloucester, who was about to become the king's son-in-law. Temporary supplies were obtained by a heavy tallage on the boroughs and royal demesnes, but it was clear that Edward's return was urgent. He did not, however, display any undue haste but spent the whole of April at Condom in Guienne, whence, after a short visit to Bordeaux, he removed his court to Condac.

At last, at the beginning of July the king started on his return journey, visiting famous shrines and relics, such as "the tear of Christ" at Vendôme, the Crown of Thorns and Nail at St. Denis and the head of John the Baptist at Amiens. Boulogne was reached early in August and on 12 August 1289 Edward crossed from Wissant to Dover and landed once more in his kingdom after more than three years' absence. At Dover the little Prince Edward and his sisters were waiting to meet their royal and affectionate parents. The court moved at once to Canterbury and thence, after visits and offerings had been paid to the relics of St. Thomas and the other shrines in the cathedral and at St. Augustine's, to Leeds Castle. Edward, who seems to have had little liking for London, displayed no anxiety to visit the capital but crossed over by Tilbury into Essex and spent the early part of September hunting at Rayleigh and Woodham Ferrers. On his way to Bury St. Edmund's he spent three days at Nayland and while there his consort, the gracious Eleanor, made him the generous gift of a thousand marks. Such a sum, however welcome, would not go far towards supplying the needs of the king, who at the time of his landing in England owed over £100,000 to the Italian merchants and bankers. Edward recognised that the time was not opportune for an appeal to the nation for further grants and that it would be well first to appease the general discontent by popular measures. After a visit, therefore, to the Blessed Virgin of Walsingham, a shrine for which he professed particular veneration, he made his way slowly to Westminster, where he was received with the usual display of magnificence on 11 October. His stay was brief, only extending over four days, but was marked by the establishment of a special commission, presided over by Burnel, Bishop of Bath, and the Earl of Lincoln, to hear all complaints relative to the conduct of the royal officials during the king's absence in Aquitaine. Already, on 24 September, Thomas de Weyland had been suspended from his office of Chief Justice of the Common Pleas; enquiries were now made into a murder in Norfolk alleged to have been committed by his retainers with his connivance. Conscious of guilt, he fled to Bury St. Edmund's and took refuge in the convent of the Friars Minors at Babwell; here, by the irony of justice, he became the victim of one of his own judicial decrees, for he had laid down the rule that if a malefactor remained in sanctuary for more than forty days without abjuring the realm, at the expiration of that term the secular authorities might prohibit any food and drink being brought to him. Accordingly the convent was surrounded and all supplies intercepted. After a short time all the friars save four abandoned their house and in the end, after living on vegetables and herbs "like a beast", Weyland surrendered and the faithful four abjured the realm and retired to Ireland. Weyland had at one time been in minor orders but had afterwards married; he now, however, endeavoured to claim the benefit of clergy at the expense of his wife's honour and it throws an unpleasant light on the superior value attached by the Church to its privileges than to morality that so upright a man as Archbishop Pecham should have written to King Edward asking him to be merciful towards Weyland on the ground that although he had kept two gentlewomen in succession as his mistresses he had never married them canonically. The Archbishop's plea was not accepted, the ex-justice was only allowed to save his life by abjuring the realm and forfeiting all his property, valued at 100,000 marks, though the rights of his wife and son in certain of his estates were afterwards recognised. Another prominent offender was Adam de Stratton, Baron of the Exchequer, who just ten years earlier had got into trouble for forgery but had then purchased pardon. On 20 October his London house was seized and the enormous hoard of £12,650 (equivalent to at least a quarter of a million of modern money) was discovered and confiscated. Rumour also said that a silken pouch was found containing human nail parings and hairs and the feet of toads and moles, clear evidence of devilish dealings and black magic. In his case the plea of clergy could not be denied and although his lay property, to the value of £50,000, was seized his clerical fees could not be touched, but he was himself condemned to perpetual imprisonment in the Tower. A similar sentence was passed on Henry de Bray, the Escheator, convicted of rape and other crimes, and the disgrace so worked upon his mind that he first endeavoured to drown himself by flinging himself out of the barge in which he was being taken to the Tower, and afterwards tried to dash out his brains against the walls of his cell. Ralph de Hengham, Chief Justice of the King's Bench, was fined 2,000 marks and dismissed from office, and heavy fines were levied

upon a number of other offending justices, including
Solomon of Rochester, who was poisoned four years
later by the vicar of Snodland, at the instigation, rumour
had it, of the Bishop of Rochester.

Having vindicated the claims of justice, thereby gaining
a certain amount of popularity and also of money,
Edward was free to turn his attention to domestic affairs,
including the betrothal or marriage of three of his
children. Of these three matrimonial alliances by far the
most important was that arranged for his infant son and
heir. It has already been mentioned that Alexander III
of Scotland had died in March 1286; as he had left no
surviving children his little granddaughter, Margaret,
daughter of King Eric of Norway, was the heir to the
Scottish throne and as such she was recognized by the
greater part of the Scots, her only opponent being
Robert Bruce of Annandale, grandson of David, brother
of William the Lion, who claimed to have been nominated
by Alexander II as heir to the throne prior to the birth of
Alexander III. Bruce's claim was not taken very seriously
and the regency council appointed on Margaret's behalf
had little difficulty in controlling the realm. Edward was
quick to see that in the marriage of Margaret to his son
Edward lay the solution of many problems. The principality of Wales had been extinguished and united to
England by force; Ireland was in as quiet and submissive
a state as could be expected of that unruly island; if
Scotland could be brought under the English crown by
marriage the English kings would in future be relieved
of the fear of troubles on their own borders and would
have a freer hand for pursuing those schemes of continental aggrandisement which were the ambition and
bane of all our medieval monarchs. Edward went to work
with quiet tact, first cultivating good relations with
Norway and with the Scottish regency, and it was not
until after his return to England that actual negotiations were opened for the marriage. Even then no open

reference to Prince Edward was made in the treaty signed at Salisbury on 6 November 1289 by the representatives of England, Scotland and Norway; it was only stipulated that Margaret should be sent over from Norway in the course of the next twelve months free from any contract of marriage and Edward on his part promised that if Scotland were in a tranquil state he would hand her over to the Scots, on condition that they should not arrange any marriage for her without the consent of himself and of the King of Norway. The true meaning of this treaty of Salisbury, which was confirmed by the Scottish parliament in the following March, is shown by the fact that within a few days of its execution Pope Nicholas IV granted a dispensation for the marriage of young Edward and the little queen. Finally, in July 1290, an agreement for the marriage was drawn up and ratified by both parties, by which the rights of the Scots were carefully safeguarded; the laws and customs of Scotland were to be maintained unaltered, the courts, feudal and legal, of the two countries were to be kept separate, and in the event of Margaret dying without issue the Scottish crown should pass to the right heir and remain independent.

Before these negotiations had been brought to this successful conclusion two other marriages had taken place in the royal family. On 30 April 1290 Joan of Acre was married to Gilbert, Earl of Gloucester. The earl, head of the ancient family of Clare, with great estates in England, Wales and Ireland, was the most powerful and wealthy, and therefore the most dangerous member of the baronage. In order to bring him under control Edward determined to bind him with the golden chains of a royal alliance and accordingly, after the earl had gone through the necessary preliminaries of obtaining a divorce from his first wife, Alais de Lusignan, and a dispensation for his marriage to Joan, the hand of that princess, destined originally for Hartman of Hapsburg, was bestowed upon him at Westminster. As one condition of the marriage Edward had caused Earl Gilbert to surrender all his estates, receiving them back to hold for life, with remainder to Joan and the heirs of her body, and he also made him swear to maintain the succession to the throne of the young Prince Edward and, in the event of his death, of the king's elder daughter Eleanor and her heirs in priority to Joan. The whole incident was typical of Edward's policy and methods, alike in the use of his children as political pawns and in his skilful neutralising of potential opposition by the judicious distribution of favours accompanied by the exaction of equivalent advantages. The king had come up to London only two days before the marriage of his daughter, going out of his way from Woodstock first to visit his mother and daughter at Amesbury and next to preside over a tournament at Winchester, given, no doubt, in honour of the approaching nuptials. He now made an unusually long stay in his capital, being there for eight weeks, until 23 June, when he retired to his Essex hunting seat of Havering-atte-Bower for some ten days, returning in time for the marriage of his daughter Margaret with John, son of the Duke of Brabant, on 9 July. While Joan of Acre had reached the comparatively mature age of nineteen Margaret was not quite fifteen, her husband being some five years older. Their engagement had been lengthy, dating back to 1278 when the bride to be was only three years old, and for the last five years young John of Brabant had been resident at the English court, developing his natural aptitude for sport and martial exercises. The dower to be bestowed upon the bride was considerable and the political value of the alliance great, and in contrast to the almost private marriage of Joan the marriage of Margaret was made the occasion for pageantry and display on a scale which eclipsed anything of the kind previously known. The abbey and the palace were thronged with nobles and ladies, the voices and instruments of more than four hundred minstrels and musicians filled the air, buffoons cracked jokes which made up in broadness what they lacked in point. All day long processions rode and marched with dance and song through the courts of the palace and the streets of the city. The Duke of Brabant had in his train eighty knights and sixty ladies, in rich attire whose strange fashion excited much remark, the young Prince Edward rode with eighty knights, the Earl of Gloucester with a hundred and three knights and, in compliment to his royal bride, sixty ladies, the Earl Marshal and Earl Warenne had forty-eight knights apiece and if the Earl of Oxford was content with a modest retinue of twelve it was acknowledged on all hands that his were the most magnificent of all in their array. Seven hundred knights and ladies and nearly a thousand citizens of London completed the gorgeous pageant. Three times during the day did all the performers change their proudery, the most magnificent costumes being, no doubt, reserved for the sumptuous banquet in Westminster Hall, of which one feature was a wonderful model of a castle most cunningly constructed by Master John Brodeye, Prince Edward's cook, which was borne into the great Hall and set before the queen.

But festivities and gaiety were not allowed to hold sway to the exclusion of other more weighty matters. On the day before the marriage ceremony there was published the chief work of the Trinity session of parliament, the Statute called, from its opening words, *Quia Emptores*, by which sub-infeudation and the creation of new manors was checked. While London was still thronged with the nobles who had come up for the royal wedding and were now waiting to attend the parliament summoned for 15 July, the strenuous Archbishop Pecham took the opportunity to preach a crusade. Moved by his eloquence many magnates took the vow of the cross, among whom were the Earl of Gloucester and his countess, Thomas Bek, Bishop of St. David's, and Sir Otes de Graundson, who had just returned from a special mission to the papal court in connection with the marriage of Prince Edward and Margaret of Scotland. Of these, Sir Otes set out for the Holy Land almost immediately, taking with him on the king's behalf money and the promise of further assistance: but for all his high-sounding name he made little noise in the theatre of war* and was unable to stave off the fall of Acre in the following year, 1291. Edward seized the opportunity of this revival of crusading enthusiasm to publish an edict decreeing the banishment of all Jews from the kingdom. They were given three months in which to collect their debts and make their arrangements for leaving the country and orders were given to ensure that they were not maltreated or robbed, but any Jew who remained in England after the beginning of November 1290 would be put to death. This decree was the most universally popular act of Edward's reign. The Jews were uniformly detested throughout the realm as enemies of the Faith and still more as devourers of their neighbour's substance. Although since the rise of the Lombard and other Italian bankers the Jews had lost their monopoly of ready money they were still supreme as capitalists outside the court and the ranks of the greater nobility, and although Edward in 1275 had prohibited them from practising usury it is pretty clear that the prohibition had been practically ignored. Their banishment was in accordance not only with the popular desires but also with Edward's whole policy towards the hated race. Under earlier kings, and especially Henry III, they had become a privileged people, under the direct protection of the king; the change of their position under his son may be indicated by a story which relates how a shifty Jew being impleaded by a knight during Edward's absence in Gascony produced a charter of Henry III by which Jews need only plead before the king in person; Edward, refusing to annul his father's acts, blandly

---

* *Otho de Grandisono, mutato cognomine, in congressu militari parvum fecit sonum.*

proposed to make matters fair by excusing Christians from answering Jews except before himself, and the Jew hastily abandoned his charter. One of Edward's earliest acts as king had been to insist that all Jews, of either sex, should wear the distinguishing badge of yellow cloth in a prominent position. Then in 1280 he ordered the sheriffs to compel Jews to attend sermons by Friars Preachers, in the hope that they might be converted; and in order to encourage their conversion he altered the old law by which the whole property of a convert went to the king and allowed the convert to retain half, applying the other half to the maintenance of the House of Converts in London, where they were to be taught trades or trained as clergy. The next year we find Pecham writing to Edward asking that measures might be taken against converts who had relapsed to Judaism, as although it was not possible to compel Jews to become Christians, when they had once accepted the Faith they could be compelled to remain in it. The archbishop at the same time was taking measures to prevent the building of new synagogues in London and in all his anti-Jewish measures he had the support of the king and still more of the Queen Mother, Eleanor of Provence, whose hatred of Jews was very pronounced. The proceedings against the Jews for clipping coins and their general arrest and fine in 1287 have already been referred to. The immediate sequel of Edward's renewal of his perennial vow of crusade in 1287 had been the expulsion of the Jews from Gascony, and it is some evidence of Edward's sincerity that he divided the money obtained from such property as they left behind them among the four orders of Friars in Aquitaine. In his banishment of the Jews from England, also, he acted with a fairness and consideration which, in view of the ideals of that period, might be called scrupulous. The exiles were allowed and even assisted to collect and remove their treasure and were protected from the malevolence of the common people. When the captain of a Kentish ship tricked his wealthy Jewish passengers into landing on a mud flat at low tide and, bidding them call upon the God of Moses who divided the Red Sea, pushed off and left them to drown, the king, far from rewarding him, caused the captain and his crew to be hanged. There does not appear to be any means of ascertaining with any degree of accuracy the number of Jews who were thus expelled from England but in view of the continuously hostile attitude of the authorities to them during the previous eighteen years their numbers, never very great, must have dwindled and the statement of contemporary chroniclers that 16,511 Jews left at this time must be a gross exaggeration, in spite of the appearance of accuracy lent by the odd eleven.

Thanks to the popularity of his policy in banishing the Jews Edward had little difficulty in persuading the parliament that met at Clipstone, a royal hunting seat in Nottinghamshire, in September to make him a grant of a subsidy of a fifteenth, the clergy subsequently granting a tenth of their spiritualities. The king might well have believed that Fortune was smiling upon him; his realms, continental and insular, were at peace and tranquil, foreign relations were satisfactory, his matrimonial schemes had gone well; there seemed no cloud on the political horizon. But in truth the wheel had begun to turn; for just half the destined period of his reign Edward's fortunes had risen steadily, but now they had attained their highest point and after a brief period of rest began to fall. The popularity gained by his expulsion of the Jews was quickly lost by the severity with which the subsidy of a fifteenth was levied, a severity the more felt from this being the first of a long series of years in which the harvests were deficient or inadequate. On 7 October 1290 the Bishop of St. Andrews wrote to Edward with the grave news that the little Queen Margaret of Scotland, on her way from Norway to

England, had died, and urging that the king should come immediately to the Border to settle the succession to the Scottish crown and prevent civil war and anarchy. The news reached Edward while he was in Derbyshire and he hastened back to Clipstone to meet his parliament and concert measures to deal with the unforeseen crisis. Although he must have seen that the position was serious it was impossible for him to realise the disastrous effect that the death of the Maid of Norway was to have upon the history of England. The discussion of hypothetical history is not very profitable, but it may be pointed out that if the marriage planned between Margaret and Edward had been consummated the union of England and Scotland might have been anticipated by several centuries, the wearisome and disastrous wars between those two kingdoms would at least have been avoided, and also the Hundred Years' War with France, arising out of Edward's actual marriage with Isabel of France. Had Margaret lived Bannockburn, Crécy and Agincourt would never have been fought. For a month King Edward remained at Clipstone and just as he was preparing to move northwards news reached him that Queen Eleanor had been taken seriously ill. She seems to have been on her way to Lincoln, possibly preceding her husband in his journey to the Scottish Border, when she developed fever. At the little village of Harby she was taken into the house of Richard de Weston, and there on 20 November, the eighteenth anniversary of his accession to the throne, the king joined her. For a week she lingered, but on 28 November 1290 she died. Her body was at once embalmed and carried to Lincoln Cathedral where it lay in state till 4 December; it was then carried in slow procession through Northampton, Dunstable and St. Albans to London. Here it was placed first in the Priory of the Holy Trinity and on the following days in the Franciscan and Dominican Friaries. On Sunday 17 December the body of the beloved queen was buried with solemn pomp

G

in Westminster Abbey, near the shrine of St. Edward and
the tomb to which the body of Henry III had been removed in the previous May; her heart was at the same
time entrusted to the Friars Preachers, to whom she had
herself early in the year given £100 to build a chapel for
its reception.

Eleanor of Castile is the most attractive personality in
the long list of English queens, her only rival being
Philippa of Hainault. Something of her charm and
fascination breathes from the beautiful effigy made for her
tomb by William Torel, though this is admittedly an
ideal rather than an actual portrait, and a little light is
thrown upon her character by casual references in
chronicles and records. Her marriage to Edward, like all
royal marriages, had been a matter of policy, but it had
developed into a real union of affection, and whether
the popular story of her having saved her husband from
the effects of the assassin's dagger by sucking the poison
out of his wounds is literally true or not, its occurrence
in contemporary literature is evidence that her devotion
towards him was a matter of common knowledge. She
was his constant companion throughout her life and his
love for her continued till her death, as Edward himself
recorded when writing to the Abbot of Cluny to desire
his prayers for her soul. A good wife and an affectionate
mother, Eleanor was also a popular queen; kind and
thoughtful for those about her, generous to the poor and
tender to the afflicted, she won the hearts of the people, at
first prejudiced against her. Shortly after she first returned to England from Palestine as queen she was on a
visit to St. Albans; at the time the townspeople were
struggling to overthrow the Abbey's monopolies of
grinding corn and fulling cloth and they determined to
enlist the queen's sympathies on their side. The abbot,
however, knowing that they were waiting for her on the
main road, brought her to the abbey by another route;
but the women, "whose attack was to be feared, since it

is hard to appease the anger of women," discovered the trick and ran round to meet her, crying out against the abbot's oppression. Eleanor at once stopped her carriage, rebuked the abbot for trying to keep the women away from her, and caused one of them to be brought to her: —fortunately for the abbot the poor woman was so over-whelmed by the presence of royalty that she was quite unable to say what was the matter. As a daughter of the splendour-loving Spaniards Eleanor seems to have had a full appreciation of magnificence and display; her purchases of plate, jewels and artistic treasures were large and varied, including not only precious stones but such more uncommon objects as Venetian glasses, articles of amber, jet and coral, dishes of the famous Damascus metal work and Moorish majolica, if we may so interpret the earthenware platters, saucers and jars "of outlandish colour" (*extranei coloris*) bought for her at Portsmouth from a Spanish ship. From this same ship were bought quantities of figs, raisins, dates, pomegranates, lemons and oranges, and there is other evidence that she was very fond of fruit. And it would seem that she was interested not only in the eating but in the growing of fruit, as in 1280 she obtained from France a quantity of grafts of the Blandurel, or *blanc durel*, apple for her garden at Langley and on her return from Aquitaine in 1289 she brought back with her to Langley certain Aragonese gardeners. We may also credit her with some literary taste, as she kept in her retinue a writer and an illuminator of books and is found buying not only books of devotion but also such works as *un romanz de Isembart*, which she caused to be re-written and illuminated, while from the purchase of a set of writing tablets for her daughter Eleanor we may perhaps conclude that she surpassed most women of her time in being able to write. Of her practice of the more common feminine accomplishments there is evidence in the fact that only a few weeks before her death a messenger was sent down to

Aylsham, the centre of the English linen manufacture, to obtain weaving instruments for her use.

The death of his beloved queen was a great blow to Edward and a week after her funeral, on Christmas Eve, he went into retirement at Ashridge, in the college of canons, or *Bons Hommes*, founded by his cousin the Earl of Cornwall. Here he remained for five weeks, going thence to Eynsham and paying a short visit in the middle of February to his mother, now growing old and feeble, at Amesbury. The settlement of the Scottish succession had now become of pressing importance; the regents, led by Bishop Fraser of St. Andrews, were willing to submit the decision to the arbitrament of Edward and he himself welcomed the opportunity of establishing his claim to the overlordship of Scotland. Accordingly in the middle of March 1291 he moved northwards, summoning the claimants to the throne and the Scottish representatives, as well as a number of English magnates, to meet him at the border castle of Norham. Here they assembled on 10 May, in the parish church, but to Edward's preliminary demand that they should recognise him as overlord of Scotland, supported though it was by precedents for which the chronicles of the English monastic houses had been ransacked, the Scottish representatives would not at first accede. After, however, a postponement of three weeks, seeing no other solution of their difficulties, the magnates accepted his terms and the protest of the more independent commoners, or gentry, was overruled. Each of the claimants in turn then declared his willingness to accept the decision of Edward as suzerain of Scotland, Edward himself undertook to maintain peace and do justice, and arbitrators were selected to constitute the court. Although some dozen claims had been put in, only three had any substantial basis; these were those of the representatives of the three daughters and heirs of David, Earl of Huntingdon, brother of William the Lion. John de Balliol was grandson of the eldest daughter, Robert

Bruce son of the second, and John de Hastings grandson of the third daughter. Practically the choice lay between Balliol as representative of the elder line and Bruce as nearer in blood, being grandson instead of great-grandson, to David; the Hastings claim could only be upheld if it were decided that the kingdom was a fief partable between co-heirs, in which case he would be entitled to one third. Ignoring this last argument, King Edward caused Balliol and Bruce to name forty arbitrators apiece, to whose number he himself added twenty-four; the list was drawn up on 5 June and next day Edward caused the competitors to give him seisin of all the land and castles of Scotland, which he undertook to return to the successful candidate within two months of his election. In virtue of this act of seisin the regency council was dissolved but was at once reappointed, with the addition of two English members. The Scottish constables were also for the moment retained in all the castles, but in July the king went on a progress, visiting Edinburgh, Stirling, St. Andrews, Perth and Roxburgh and installing in those and nearly a score of other castles English constables. On 2 August he was at Berwick and the next day the proceedings opened, the twelve candidates putting in their claims in detail. On 12 August Edward adjourned the court for ten months, till 2 June 1292, and hastened south. When the cause was resumed on the appointed day the question was practically limited to the relative claims of Balliol and Bruce. The former was undoubtedly the heir by English law, the latter had the better claim under Scottish custom and had also been recognised by Alexander II, when that monarch was childless, as his successor. It was therefore essential to decide whether English or Scottish law was to predominate, but on this point the arbitrators declined to pronounce an opinion, neither party caring to commit themselves to a course which might damage their candidate. After various adjournments Edward caused his own arbitrators to hear the arguments of the two candidates and questioned them individually as to what laws they considered should apply; not unnaturally they all agreed that the rules of English law were applicable to the descent of the Scottish crown. The eighty Scottish arbitrators dissented feebly from this view but admitted that if a case arose for which the Scottish law had not provided, then the English king might legislate to meet the case. On 5 November decision was given against Bruce; to this verdict Balliol's forty arbitrators naturally agreed and those appointed by Bruce seem to have given a reluctant assent. After discussing the divisibility of the kingdom and the claims of the other candidates the king pronounced that John de Balliol was the true heir to the Scottish throne and two days later seisin of the realm was made to him and the castles put into his hands. The seal used during the vacancy of the throne was broken and sent to the English Treasury to be preserved, with a roll on which Edward had caused a full account of the proceedings to be entered, judiciously garbled in such a manner as to make it appear that the Scots had recognised his claim not only to the suzerainty but also to the actual throne of Scotland. On St. Andrew's Day, 30 November 1292 John de Balliol was crowned king and enthroned on the famous Stone of Destiny at Scone and on 26 December he did homage to Edward at Newcastle for the realm of Scotland.

So far Edward's actions had borne at least the appearance of justice and it would have been well if he had been contented with the advantages which he had gained; but he had determined to bring Scotland under the English yoke and seems deliberately to have embarked upon the policy of bullying the unfortunate King John into rebellion in order to have a pretext for the seizure of his throne. The means selected was by insisting upon the right of hearing appeals from the Scottish courts. The first of these was a case, insignificant in itself, in which one Roger Bartholomew, probably by Edward's contrivance, lodged an appeal to the English court on 7 December 1292, which appeal Edward at once accepted. To Balliol's objection that this was contrary to the Treaty of Brigham, by which no Scot was to be compelled to plead out of the realm, Edward replied by stating quite plainly that circumstances were altered, that promises made during the vacancy of the Scottish throne no longer applied and that no promise or treaty should prevent him from exercising his right as overlord to hear appeals. Further, on 2 January 1293, he compelled Balliol to cancel the treaty. With the result of Edward's policy in this matter of the appeals we shall have to deal in the next chapter.

On the occasion of the first adjournment of the court in August 1291 Edward had hastened down to Amesbury for the funeral of his mother, who had died on 25 June. Her embalmed body, by the king's desire, had been left unburied until he could be present. Eleanor of Provence was a kindly, narrow and commonplace woman, devout to a degree which to modern ideas would seem bigoted but was admirable in the eyes of her contemporaries, affectionate, and even devoted, to her husband, children and relations. Her injudicious devotion to the welfare of her many foreign relatives had rendered her un- popular with her English subjects and had been disas- trous to the kingdom, but she retained the affection of her son till her death. In her letters to Edward, a con- siderable number of which have survived, we find constant evidence of her kindly interest in those who required help:—at one time she writes on behalf of a widow whose heiress daughter is in ward to another lady, asking that she may see her child occasionally; more frequently the object of her intervention is a cleric or a monastery, the Abbot of Medmenham, "the poorest abbey of Cistercians in England", the Prior of Michelham, involved in a troublesome suit with a neighbouring abbot, or the Prior- elect of Malvern who has been imprisoned by the Abbot of Westminster. Occasionally a more personal note is struck, as when she commends to him Aumary Peche, whose father Bartholomew Peche "took care of you when you were a child", or expresses her pleasure at hearing that he likes the new house at Bindon which she has given him, or indulges in rather obscure jokes about some fine, fat cranes which he had sent her with a facetious enquiry as to whether she would rather have the heads without the bodies or the bodies without the heads. As late as September 1290 she writes a rather fussy letter to say that she hears he intends taking Prince Edward with him to the north (no doubt to meet the Maid of Norway, his affianced bride) and urging that he should leave him in some place with a good, temperate climate, as she always found herself that the bad air of the north made her ill. The suggestion that Eleanor was asthmatic might be supported by the fact that in 1257 she left Nottingham Castle because she could not endure the fumes of the pit coal burnt in the town, and also by a letter in which she mentions that she has left Gillingham and gone to Marlborough "because of the chilliness of the air and the heavy mists which rise in the evenings".

From Amesbury King Edward went westwards to Abergavenny to enquire into a quarrel, amounting practically to a private war, between his son-in-law the Earl of Gloucester, and the Earl of Hereford. Gloucester had been the aggressor, his men having on three occasions raided the Bohun lands of Brecon, robbed a church and driven off quantities of cattle, their master receiving a third of the spoil; he now endeavoured to evade trial by pleading the privilege of the March, but both he and Hereford, whose men had retaliated in spite of the royal prohibition, were condemned to prison and to loss of their liberties; in view, however, of the fact that Earl Gilbert was the king's son-in-law and the Earl of Hereford had married a relation of Queen Eleanor the sentence of imprisonment was commuted for heavy fines, 10,000 marks in the case of Gloucester and 1,000 marks in the case of his less guilty rival. On 21 November Edward was again at Amesbury, where he received the casket containing his mother's heart, which he took with him to London; and on the anniversary of the death of Eleanor of Castile, observed with great solemnity at Westminster, the heart of Eleanor of Provence was buried at the Friars Preachers in accordance with the custom then prevalent.* The incident gave an opening for a monastic chronicler to sneer at the hated friars as always scrambling for portions of the bodies of the great and wealthy dead, like dogs gathering hungrily round a carcase.

In addition to his wife and his mother Edward lost about the same time two faithful ministers. His Treasurer, the upright but harsh and haughty John de Kirkby, Bishop of Ely, died early in the year 1290; as the man responsible for wringing money out of his master's reluctant subjects he was naturally unpopular, and the clergy, whose purses had suffered to an unprecedented extent at his hands, compared him to St. John Baptist, with the difference that whereas the one prepared the way for his Lord in the desert the other prepared the way of his king into Hell. More serious was the death, on 25 October 1292, of Robert Burnel, Bishop of Bath and Wells, who had been Chancellor for the exceptional term of eighteen years, during which he had served his master faithfully, directed his policy with singular wisdom and yet had, by his tact and charm, retained the affection of the people. Before the end of the same year, on 8 December 1292, died John Pecham, Burnel's supplanter in the Primacy, an honourable, hard-working, but not always tactful man. In April of the previous year Pope Nicholas IV had died, urging to the last the cause of a crusade, which, a month later, by the fall of Acre on 18 May 1291, ceased to possess even a shadowy claim to realisation.

* When the heart of Eleanor of Castile was buried at the Friars Preachers the hearts of her son Alphonso and of Sir John de Vescy were also buried there, and in December 1291 the heart of Henry III was given to the Abbess of Fontevrault to be interred in her abbey.

# Chapter Six

# France and Scotland

After King John had returned to the insecure dignity of his Scottish throne the English court left Newcastle, early in January 1293, and moved slowly southwards. Easter (29 March) was kept at Harleston in Suffolk and visits were paid to Ely and St. Albans before King Edward reached Westminster on 16 April. Here he remained for the whole of May and June in consultation with his parliament on matters of finance and foreign affairs. In spite of the care which he had displayed in avoiding quarrels with France and the correctness of his official attitude towards his overlord the French king, it was becoming increasingly clear that relations between the two countries, invariably and inevitably strained, were in an exceptionally dangerous state. However correct the attitude of their lords, the common people of the rival nationalities made no pretence of mutual tolerance. The English, and especially the sailors of the Cinque Ports, a set of bold ruffians, half traders and half pirates, displayed an insular contempt for the foreigners, to which the French retorted by declaring that the English had tails and were more beasts than men. Towards the Gascons, as subjects of the English king, the French displayed enmity while the men of the Cinque Ports were almost equally willing to plunder them or to join with them in an attack on their common enemies. The great wine trade, of which Bayonne and Bordeaux were the centres, drew the shipping of Normandy and

England to those ports and quarrels, piracy and murder were incidents too common as a rule to lead to serious consequences. At last in 1292 an insignificant struggle between an English and a Norman sailor, in which the Norman was killed with his own sword, led to the adoption by the French, by the inspiration either of King Philip or of his brother Charles of Valois, of a systematic privateering warfare against English ships. Proclamations by the Constable of Bordeaux and by the French and English kings enjoining the observation of peace upon their subjects were ignored, the Norman ships ostensibly trading to Bayonne for wine were converted into men-of-war by the erection of fore-, stern- and top-castles and, keeping together, constituted a formidable fleet which captured, plundered and sank English ships, hanging their crews from the yard-arm side by side with the ships' dogs. The Gascons retorted by a raid on La Rochelle and the murder of various officials and of merchants who were rash enough to speak the northern dialect in the streets of Bayonne, while the English attacked and destroyed French and Flemish shipping in the harbour at Sluys. At last on 15 May 1293 a pitched battle was fought, apparently by prearrangement, off St. Mahé between English, Irish and Gascons on the one hand and the Norman fleet, assisted by Flemish and Genoese ships, on the other. All the ships were in full battle array, flying the long red streamers, or *baucans*, which signified that no quarter would be given and that the fight should be to the finish. The English fleet numbered about eighty vessels while their enemies were quite twice as numerous, but probably smaller. After a desperate struggle the French were completely defeated and their fleet practically annihilated. King Philip was naturally incensed and sent a peremptory demand for satisfaction and the return of such ships and goods as had been carried off. Edward had already sent his brother Edmund and the Earl of Lincoln to consult with Philip as to the best way of putting an end to the quarrels between the mariners of England and Normandy, and he now replied with dignity and courtesy that his courts were open to all complainants and that he would gladly submit any disputed points to arbitration or allow the whole matter to be placed before the pope, "whose mission it is to encourage peace between kings and kingdoms", or, as the papacy was vacant, before the cardinals. At the same time he sent a message to the barons of the Cinque Ports urging them to be content with the victory that they had gained and to cease from molesting the Normans. The Portsmen replied by laying the whole blame on the Normans, and to the suggestion that they should surrender their prizes answered that for an action fought under the *baucan* no restitution or amends were ever made; they added, in true Viking spirit, that if wrong were done them they would abandon their homes and take to the sea. Philip's attitude was even less satisfactory, as he reiterated his complaints against the Gascon sailors and added a series of charges relating to the suppression of appeals from the courts of the Duchy of Aquitaine to his own court, ending by citing Edward to appear before him in person at Paris.

The citation and the raising of the question of appeals were well timed and came at a singularly inconvenient moment for Edward. Pursuing his policy, to which we referred at the end of the last chapter, of bringing the Scottish crown completely under his own control and rendering the position of King John either insignificant or impossible, Edward at his Whitsun parliament in 1293 had drawn up certain regulations or orders by which not only were appeals from the Scottish court to be heard in England, contrary to all precedent, but the Scottish king was made a party to all such appeals, was bound to attend at their hearing, in person or by an attorney, and was rendered personally responsible for any damages or amercements resulting therefrom. Having himself stretched the theory of feudal overlordship to such an extraordinary degree Edward was in no position to dispute the claims of Philip, and had therefore to trust to the diplomacy and tact of his brother Edmund and the influence of Edmund's wife, Blanche of Navarre, as mother of the French queen. Meanwhile Edward, after spending most of July at Canterbury and August in the neighbourhood of Winchester, moved down to Bristol, where at the end of September his eldest daughter Eleanor was married to Henry, Count of Bar. Eleanor had for many years been engaged to Alphonso of Aragon and, although the determined opposition of successive popes to the match had prevented the marriage, it would seem that her betrothal had been considered by Edward an obstacle to her contracting any other alliance until the death of Alphonso, in 1291. Now that trouble with France seemed inevitable and it was important to secure allies her hand was hastily bestowed upon Henry, Count of Bar, a lordship upon the borders of Champagne. As a further mark of favour the count's brother Theobald was given the valuable living of Pagham, then in the king's hands owing to the vacancy of the see of Canterbury, the new archbishop Robert Winchelsey not having yet received the papal confirmation. In October the newly married Count and Countess went on a visit to Prince Edward at Mortlake while the king made his way to Westminster for the autumn parliament. At this parliament King John of Scotland was present as a party to the appeals made from his courts by Macduff, Aufrike heiress of Man, the Abbot of Reading and others. He, however, declined to plead or to acknowledge the legality of the proceedings and could with difficulty be persuaded even to compromise so far as to ask for an adjournment that he might consult with his subjects on the matter.

While this parliament was sitting and Edward was thus pressing his feudal claims of suzerainty in the case of Scotland, Edmund of Lancaster was striving his hardest to extricate his royal brother from the unpleasant consequences of the French suzerainty over Aquitaine. King Philip, finding that the military resources of Gascony had been well organised by Edward's lieutenant, John St. John, was unwilling to attempt an armed invasion of Aquitaine and therefore resorted to trickery. He intimated his own personal willingness to recall the summons to Paris but declared that his nobles would not hear of such a concession; but after further negotiations, in which Queen Jeanne and the Dowager Queen Marie, widow of Philip III, played a prominent part, it was agreed that there should be a purely formal cession of Gascony, followed by a friendly meeting of the two kings at Amiens, and that the amicable understanding should be completed by the marriage of Edward with Philip's sister Margaret. Six castles were to be surrendered to Philip, twenty Gascon officials were to submit to honourable arrest, French officials were to be installed throughout the towns, with the exception of Bayonne, Bordeaux and La Réole, the administration of justice and the revenues of the Duchy were to be placed in French hands and complete seisin would thus be given to Philip for the term of forty days, at the expiration of which period he pledged his honour to return the whole to King Edward. Edmund naturally hesitated to agree to the surrender of Gascony without some guarantee of its return and the terms were therefore embodied in a secret treaty signed by Queen Jeanne, who pledged her faith for its observance. On the strength of this, Edward, who, although he could upon occasion evade an inconvenient obligation, was incapable of deliberate treachery, caused letters to be executed in his name authorising the surrender of Gascony to King Philip, and as the Chancellor, John de Langton, shrewder or more suspicious than his royal master, refused to have anything to do with such an agreement he caused Walter de Langton, Treasurer of the Wardrobe, to set his seal to

the letters on 1 January 1294. Even then Edmund
hesitated, and it was not until King Philip had paid him a
private visit and in the presence of witnesses had pledged
his royal word for the observance of the treaty and the
immediate repeal of the summons that he despatched the
letters. The order for the surrender of Gascony was received with dismay in the Duchy, but there was no
alternative; the surrender was made, St. John disbanded
his army, sold his stores and returned to England. Here
also Edward's action, taken without consulting his
barons, had given great offence and in consequence his
court in East Anglia during Lent was almost deserted
by the nobles. Early in April 1294 the king accompanied
his daughter Eleanor and her husband to Dover, from
which port they sailed on the 14th of that month.
Edward then returned to Canterbury to keep Easter and
to await the safe-conduct promised by Philip for the
meeting at Amiens. But Philip now showed his hand;
ever since the forty days had expired Edmund had been
pressing for the restoration of Gascony; at first he had
been put off with stories of political circumstances
necessitating caution and delay, but at last he was told
bluntly that the French king had no intention of giving
up anything that he had got into his hands and on 5 May
King Philip made his intentions quite clear by renewing
the citation of Edward and declaring that he had forfeited Gascony by his contumacy. This was practically
equivalent to a declaration of war; Edmund at once left
Paris and his example was followed by the English
students and other residents there; a Dominican and a
Franciscan friar were sent to Philip on Edward's behalf
to renounce his homage; the English ports were closed
against all continental traffic before the end of May and
on 2 June King John was requested to close the Scottish
ports also. King John was at this time in London attending the parliament which ratified the declaration of war
against France and he is stated to have generously put at

Edward's disposal the revenues of his English estates for
three years; the probability however is that if any such
grant was made by him it was under compulsion or else
intended to placate Edward for the refusal of any assistance
from his Scottish dominions. Other magnates, however,
were more ready to promise financial aid and a large sum
was raised by the sudden seizure, authorised by the
council, of all the wool and leather in the country and its
subsequent redemption by the merchants at an extor-
tionate figure. Money was urgently needed, not only for
the normal expenses of a great war but more particularly
for the purchase of alliances with continental rulers, such
as Adolf of Nassau, King of the Romans, Siegfried the
princely Archbishop of Cologne, the kings of Castile and
Aragon and the Count of Holland, and for the hire of
mercenaries from Burgundy and Savoy. To secure the
assistance of Guy, Count of Flanders, a marriage was proposed between Prince Edward and Philippa the Count's
daughter. In his two sons-in-law Henry of Bar and John,
now Duke of Brabant by reason of his father's death at a
tournament given in honour of the marriage of the Count
of Bar, Edward had two useful allies, but they, like the
others, required pay. In order to obtain some idea of the
bullion resources of the country Edward, immediately
after the closing of parliament at the end of June, ordered
a scrutiny of all the treasure deposited in the monasteries
and churches throughout the realm. In the absence of
banks it was at this time the custom for the wealthy to
entrust their surplus treasure, in coin or jewels, to the
security of a church, monastic or otherwise, where it
would have the protection alike of strong walls and of the
sanctity attaching to consecrated buildings and would
also as a rule be under the constant eye of a custodian.
Of these hoards, Edward now caused a duplicate in-
ventory to be made, one portion being returned into the
Exchequer and the other given to the head of the church
in which the treasure was kept. Such a measure, though it

roused great indignation, was not unjustifiable as a means of ascertaining the liabilities of the wealthier classes, often evaded, in respect to subsidies levied on movables but, not content with this, the king took the opportunity in the case of persons who owed him money or had promised loans to seize the amount of the debt or loan. He also seized the estates of the alien priories, the monastic houses directly dependent on foreign abbeys, to which they sent a portion, often the greater part, of their English revenues; by this means, therefore, Edward not only obtained money himself but also cut off supplies from entering France. His next step was to call the clergy together at Westminster on 21 September and ask for a subsidy; to this they replied with the liberal offer of two-tenths of their revenues but Edward promptly and peremptorily demanded a full half on pain of outlawry. While they were debating over this unprecedented demand in the Abbey Sir John de Havering entered and called for anyone who would oppose the king's orders to stand up that he might be known for a traitor. No one accepted the invitation and the clergy, further agitated by the sudden death of the Dean of St. Pauls, who fell in a fit at the feet of the king before he could deliver their message of remonstrance, yielded and made the required grant.

The general muster had been ordered for 30 September at Portsmouth but an advance force had been despatched some weeks before under command of John of Brittany with Sir John St. John as Seneschal of Gascony and Sir Robert Tiptoft. Contrary winds, however, had driven their ships into Plymouth and it was not until early in October that they were able to make a fresh start and it was almost the end of the month before they landed in Gascony. Meanwhile the naval defences of England had been reorganised, the ships being grouped in three fleets, of which that of the Cinque Ports and southern coast was under William de Leyburne, with the new title of

H

Admiral, the ships of Yarmouth and the eastern ports
being under John Boteturte and those of the west under
an Irish knight. But the elaborate preparations for the
Gascon expedition were suddenly brought to nought by
trouble nearer at home. Relying upon the king's sailing
with all his available troops, as arranged, on 30 September
the Welsh had plotted a final effort to regain their liberty
by a concerted rising on the previous day, Michaelmas
1294. Under Madog and Morgan, both members,
probably illegitimate, of the line of Llewelyn, a general
attack was made on the English centres; the royal castles
of Carnarvon and other strongholds were stormed and
dismantled and the estates of the Marcher lords ravaged.
Owing to the delay caused by adverse winds the fleet
was still lying at Portsmouth and Edward himself had not
left London when news arrived of this rising. He at once
countermanded the Gascon expedition, ordered an army
to assemble on the Welsh borders by the end of November
and hastily summoning a representative parliament laid
his case before them and obtained a grant of a subsidy of
a tenth from the country generally and, subsequently, of a
sixth from the cities and boroughs. An attempt by the
Earl of Lincoln to relieve Denbigh Castle resulted in a
disastrous defeat at the hands of his own Welsh tenants
on 11 November. The news of this setback must have
reached Edward just after he had left London and was on
his way to Worcester, in which city he spent the first
few days of the twenty-third year of his reign. Before
leaving for Chester he addressed to the Chapter General
of the Franciscans at Assisi a request for their prayers for
peace and quieter times. On Christmas or the following
day he entered the castle of Conway but the festival was
not observed with the feasts and banqueting usual at that
season, for, having pushed on with a small force to the
castle, the king found himself cut off from his transport
and the main body of his army by the sudden rising of the
river and was for some days besieged by the insurgents. If

not in actual danger the garrison, with their numbers suddenly increased without any proportionate increase of supplies, found themselves in considerable discomfort, food of any kind being very scanty and wine reduced to a single gallon, of which Edward magnanimously refused to avail himself, preferring to share the lot of his comrades in arms, reduced to that last extremity of the English medieval warrior, the drinking of water.

Thus terminated the year 1294, a year of ill omen and misfortunes for England. During the year war had broken out with France and with the Welsh and Scotland was in a state of ferment which augured ill for the future; clergy and laity alike had been impoverished by the demands upon their purses; such foreign trade as had not been prohibited for reasons of state had practically been extinguished by the prevalence of pirates; and the inclement weather, with constant rain and floods, had ruined the crops and sent the price of corn up to famine height. The year 1295 opened with an event of better promise. On 1 January the expeditionary force in Aquitaine, which had already recovered Oloron, Castillon, Bourg, Blaye, Podensac and Rions, obtained possession of the town of Bayonne, the castle surrendering a few weeks later. But the appearance of success was delusive; no further progress was made and in March Charles of Valois and the Constable of France, Raoul de Nesle, retook Podensac. On 7 April a mutiny of the native infantry caused John of Brittany to fly from Rions, leaving the town and a number of its English defenders to fall into the hands of the French. By the middle of the summer little beyond Bayonne and St. Sever remained in possession of the English. Meanwhile for the first three months of 1295 King Edward remained at Conway and here he received Robert Winchelsey, Archbishop of Canterbury, on his return from Rome where he had received consecration at the hands of Pope Celestine V. That pious and simple successor of St. Peter, over-whelmed by the responsibilities of his position, took the unprecedented step of resigning the papacy in December 1294 after a brief four months of office, and the official intimation of the election of his successor Benedetto Gaetani, with the title of Boniface VIII, reached Edward at Conway in March and was acknowledged by the despatch of the usual present of gold plate to the new pontiff. Early in this same month of March the Earl of Warwick inflicted a severe defeat upon the Welsh under Madog, using his crossbowmen and archers most effectually to break up the massed formations upon which they relied. A little earlier the Earl of Hereford had gained an important success at Abergavenny and by the middle of April, when the king crossed over to Anglesey to arrange for the erection of a castle at Beaumaris, the back of the rebellion had been broken and the Welsh were gladly availing themselves of Edward's clemency to make their peace with him. During the progress of the royal forces through Wales during May and June Morgan and his men, whose rising had been mainly directed against the unpopular Earl of Gloucester, were persuaded by the Earl of Warwick to make their peace with Edward. A rash promise made by the Abbot of Strata Florida that he would bring in the western insurgents not being fulfilled, the king angrily ordered the abbey to be burnt, though he afterwards disavowed the action of those who had taken him at his word. By 20 July, when Edward was back at Worcester, where he publicly proclaimed his gratitude for St. Wulfstan's assistance, Wales was once more in a state of peace, to which the final seal was set by the surrender of Madog on 30 July. Madog was committed to the Tower and some scores of Welsh hostages were distributed throughout England in various castles ranging from York to Pevensey, but Edward, in spite of the serious interference of the Welsh rising with his Gascon plans, was in a clement mood and the only victims of his anger after hostile operations had terminated were a certain Conan ap Llewelyn and two companions, taken at Brecon and hanged at Hereford.

On 2 August 1295, the day on which King Edward re-entered his capital, a French fleet made a sudden raid on Dover, plundered the town and broke into the priory, where they slew an aged and saintly monk who had remained at the altar in the infirmary chapel when his brethren had sought the security of the church tower. The townsmen quickly rallied and drove out the invaders with heavy loss and the English ships took a speedy revenge by sacking Cherbourg and ravaging the Norman coast. A great French galley which imprudently put into Hythe was captured, a proposed attack on Winchelsea by a large French squadron was hastily abandoned when the English fleet hove in view, Spanish merchant ships with valuable cargoes were brought into Sandwich and generally the English appear to have proved themselves at least the equals of their rivals on the sea. But with the news of the attack on Dover still fresh in their ears and with the story of King Philip's falseness and treachery newly expounded to them by the Earl of Lancaster the August parliament was in no mood to listen to the pleadings of the two cardinals sent by Pope Boniface to promote the cause of peace between the two realms, and they were politely dismissed on the pretext that the King of the Germans, as the chief of our allies, must first be consulted; at the same time they were authorised to arrange for a three months' truce if King Philip desired it. A fresh proof of the French king's underhand methods was now brought to light. Among the English prisoners taken at Rions was a knight, Sir Thomas de Turberville, who to regain his liberty undertook to act as a spy and an agent for the French. He was therefore allowed to return to England, where he gave out that he had escaped from prison, and being a good soldier as well as a plausible liar he was taken into favour

by Edward, from whom he endeavoured, fortunately
without success, to obtain the custody of some seaport.
Meanwhile he was trying, again without success, to
persuade Morgan to raise a fresh rebellion in Wales, and
he had also plotted to seize King Edward while he was
at Canterbury in the middle of September attending the
enthronement of Archbishop Winchelsey. A letter from
him to the Provost of Paris being intercepted the whole
plot came to light and he was executed as a traitor. More
serious danger, however, was now threatening in the
north, where Edward's policy of pinpricks had at last
driven the Scots into the arms of his enemies. Balliol's
position had become impossible and if he himself had
been prepared to sink into the position of a petty prince
his subjects were determined that Scotland should not
thus be degraded. Accordingly the Scottish parliament
in July appointed a council of twelve peers to assist, or
practically to control, their king; a marriage was arranged between the king's eldest son, Edward Balliol,
and the daughter of Charles of Valois; and all persons
whose estates and interests were predominantly English
were deprived of their Scottish possessions. Amongst
these latter was Robert Bruce of Annandale, son of the
original claimant, who had died on 31 March of this year,
and father of the younger Robert, Earl of Carrick and
eventually King of Scotland. The English king retorted
by ordering the seizure of the property of Scots within the
realm and by demanding the surrender of the castles of
Berwick, Roxburgh and Jedburgh for the term of the
war with France, as a guarantee of good faith. But just a
week after this order had been issued a definite treaty of
alliance between Scotland and France against England
was signed at Paris on 23 October 1295.

On 27 November 1295 there assembled at Westminster
a parliament to which not only the barons but the
representatives of the clergy, the shires and the boroughs
had been summoned, constituting the completest and

most representative assembly of the kind ever yet called together, and therefore regarded as a precedent and afterwards known as the Model Parliament. The chief business of this parliament was to provide supplies for the wars with France and Scotland and for this purpose subsidies were voted of an eleventh from the country generally, a seventh from the cities and boroughs and a tenth from the clergy. A small expeditionary force had been collected by the beginning of November but owing to the illness of Edmund of Lancaster, its appointed leader, it did not sail until the end of December. A few isolated successes were scored during the spring of 1296 but an attempt to seize Bordeaux having failed, Edmund fell back to Bayonne and, worn out by the worries attendant on ill success and lack of funds, died about the middle of May. In the hands of his successor in the command, the handsome and popular Earl of Lincoln, the war dragged on wearily with desultory fighting and little result till the end of the year.

Edmund "Crouchback", Earl of Leicester, Derby and Lancaster, seems to have been a popular noble of no outstanding abilities, great rather from the accident of his royal birth and his wealth than from any inherent quality. His unquestioned fidelity was his great merit in his brother's eyes and led to his being employed in a number of missions and positions of importance for which the cautious monarch hesitated to select less reliable men of greater brilliance. His loss deprived Edward of an amiable brother, a wealthy supporter and an imposing mouthpiece and reduced the already singularly small circle of the king's intimates and trusted agents. About the same time Edward also lost his uncle William de Valence, Earl of Pembroke, but he had taken little part in English politics and his place was more than filled by his son and successor Aymer de Valence. In December 1295 another of Edward's comrades in arms of the Baronial War, his son-in-law Gilbert de

Clare, Earl of Gloucester, died; a restless, impetuous, unstable man. The earl had been preceded to the grave by his brother Bogo de Clare, remarkable only as the greatest pluralist of his age, a man with more manors than manners, the incumbent, or rather the incumberer, of innumerable churches, of whose life "God knows if it was praiseworthy but it was certainly not to be paralleled." Another change of some political significance was the disgrace of William de Marchia, Bishop of Bath, his removal from the office of Treasurer and the bestowal of that office, together with the vacant see of Coventry and Lichfield, upon Walter de Langton, the most influential of the king's advisers.

Edward was at St. Albans on 1 January 1296 and from there sent out letters to the prelates requesting their prayers for the success of his Gascon expedition. Later in the month, he visited his favourite shrines of St. Edmund's and Walsingham, to which, as well as to St. Richard of Chichester, he had in the previous November sent gifts of jewels and wax. Thus spiritually fortified he moved northwards in February to York and Beverley, from which place he caused the celebrated banner of St. John to be carried to the front with his army. By 1 March he was at Newcastle with his army waiting, theoretically, for Balliol to come and make his peace. War had not yet actually been declared but the first step was now taken by his opponents. Robert de Ros, lord of the border fortress of Wark, being infatuated with a Scottish lady, proposed to surrender his castle to the Scots, but his brother William refused to agree and sent a message to Edward. A small force sent to relieve Wark was cut up by the Scots in a night attack and the king, more pleased by the fact that his enemies had put themselves in the wrong by beginning hostilities than perturbed by the loss of his men, moved with his army to Wark, which he reached on 17 March. Here he remained for Easter, which this year fell on Lady Day, and three days later he

crossed the Tweed to Coldstream, the Bishop of Durham
with his contingent crossing farther east near Norham.
His advance had been anticipated by a raid into England
by the Scots under the seven earls (Buchan, Menteith,
Strathearn, Lennox, Ross, Atholl, and Mar) on Easter
Monday. Ravaging, burning and plundering, they rushed
on Carlisle. Finding the main bridge strongly held by a
force of archers they crossed the Eden by a ford at
Rickerby and burnt the suburbs of the city. One of their
spies also, escaping from custody, kindled a fire which
consumed a large part of the city. Under cover of this
diversion an assault was attempted, but although the
men of Carlisle were mostly engaged in dealing with
the fire the strength of the walls and the valour of the
women, who flung stones and missiles from the parapets,
disappointed the invaders of their prey and they turned
back and re-entered Scotland on the same day as King
Edward.

Pitching his camp at Hutton, Edward himself rode to
the gates of Berwick and summoned the town to surrender. To his demands the citizens replied with insolent
derision and defiance, bidding him break his way in if he
wanted to enter. Plans had been made for a concerted
attack by the land forces and by the fleet of the Cinque
Ports, but early next morning when the king was re-
viewing his troops and dubbing knights the Portsmen,
seeing the army apparently in battle array, delivered their
attack prematurely. Several ships and a number of men
were lost but Edward hastened to bring up his forces.
It would seem that Edward employed the device which
had proved so successful at Evesham and advanced with
the banners of his Scottish adversaries displayed; or
perhaps the men of Fife who constituted the garrison
were unaware of the presence on the English side of the
Scottish nobles of the Bruce faction—Bruce of Annandale, his son the Earl of Carrick, the Earls of March
and Angus and others—whose banners they saw and

recognised. Whatever the cause, the English forces were mistaken for the relieving army promised by Balliol and almost before the error had been discovered they had swept irresistibly over the insufficient defences of the town and were slaying and plundering in the streets. Almost alone of the townsmen a little group of Flemings, ensconced in their stone-built gild-hall, put up a stout resistance. A stray bolt shot from this Red Hall struck Richard of Cornwall, Edward's cousin, in the face and slew him. Enraged by the insults of the previous day and the death of his cousin, the usually merciful king gave orders that no quarter should be shown. The Red Hall was fired and perished with its gallant garrison, the townspeople were butchered without distinction of age or sex and it was only by the repeated prayers and supplications of the clergy that Edward was induced to stay his hand before the unfortunate population had been completely exterminated. Next day the castle was surrendered by William Douglas, and for a month Edward remained at Berwick strengthening its defences by the construction of a great fosse and even condescending to wheel a barrow himself as an example to those engaged upon the work. Here on 5 April he received the messengers of King John charged with the formal renunciation of his homage, on which he commented with scornful menace, *"A ce felon tel foli feit? S'il ne volt venir à nous nous vendrons à li."*

Three days later the Scots made a fresh raid into England, laying waste Redesdale, Cockerdale and Tyndale, vainly attacking Harbottle castle and wreaking an easier vengeance upon the monastery of Hexham, the nunnery of Lambley and the schools of Corbridge. From Lanercost Priory they fled with their booty on the mere rumour of Edward's approach. News now arrived that Earl Patrick's castle of Dunbar, which he had left in the custody of his wife when he joined King Edward, had been occupied by a strong force of Scots. The Earl of

Warenne was at once sent forward to invest the castle, whose defenders sent an urgent message to Balliol, or to the council of which he was the figure-head. In response to their appeal a force, strong in numbers but weak in discipline, was despatched and came in sight of Dunbar on the morning of 27 April. John de Warenne at once advanced to meet them, leaving a small containing force of inferior troops to prevent any sally by the exultant garrison of the castle. As the English army broke up into small bodies and deployed for the purpose of crossing the intervening valley the Scots, thinking that they were taking to flight, raised shouts of victory which were suddenly silenced as their opponents reformed ranks and advanced in perfect order. At the first shock of conflict the undisciplined Scots broke and fled, Sir Patrick Graham almost alone of their leaders facing the foe and fighting manfully to the death. With the dissipation of this relieving force the fate of the castle was sealed and on the arrival of King Edward next day it was surrendered unconditionally by Richard Siward, the Constable. The Earls of Atholl, Ross and Menteith and 130 knights and esquires fell into Edward's hands and were sent into England to be distributed among the various castles throughout the realm. By this single stroke the Scots were deprived of practically all their natural leaders and the surrender of Roxburgh Castle on 8 May, followed by that of Jedburgh a fortnight later, made the disaster more complete. Edinburgh held out for five days, but Stirling was abandoned without any attempt at defence. From Stirling, where he was joined by the Earl of Ulster with an Irish contingent, Edward moved, on 21 June to Perth, where he received an embassy from Balliol begging to be allowed to make his peace with him. Accordingly on 2 July at Kincardine the unfortunate King John, in the presence of his chief supporters, the Comyns of Buchan and Badenoch, met the Bishop of Durham as Edward's representative and made an abject apology for his behaviour and surrendered the kingdom. The resignation was repeated with further formalities at Brechin three days later and he was at once taken to King Edward at Montrose. Edward could afford to be generous; he accepted the ex-king's explanation that his rebellion had been forced upon him by his subjects and treated him with liberality, merely restricting him to the district within twenty miles of London.

During July and August King Edward made a royal progress through the new realm which he believed he had won, visiting the more important cities such as Aberdeen, that "good toune upon the see", and Elgin. From Elgin, the most northerly point of his excursion, he sent forces to explore Badenoch and the mountains of Aberdeenshire while he returned by forsaken little Invercarrach, "wher ther was no more than iij houses in a rewe between too mountaignes", Brechin, the Abbey of Aberbrothock, Dundee, "the redde castell" of Baligarny to Perth. Thence, carrying away from Scone Abbey the venerated "Stone of Destiny", on which legend related that the head of the patriarch Jacob once rested and more authentic history recorded that the Scottish monarchs had been enthroned for close on five hundred years, he marched west to St. Andrews and then back through little Markinch, "wher as is but the churche and iij houses", and Dunfermline, with the tombs of the Scottish kings, to Stirling and so returned to Berwick on 23 August 1296. At Berwick he held a council of the magnates of both realms and received the personal oaths of fealty from some two thousand men whose birth or estates marked them out as representatives of the Scottish gentry. The clergy who had been deprived of their benefices for their English sympathies were reinstated, the more important castles were entrusted to English constables and the chief supporters of the late king, including the Comyns, were forbidden to return to Scotland until the war between England and France was over; but otherwise, so far as possible, little was done to disturb the existing order of things, Edward being anxious to gain the goodwill of his new subjects. John de Warenne, Earl of Surrey, was appointed Warden of Scotland, with Henry Percy as Warden of Galloway; Walter de Agmondesham was made Chancellor, William de Ormesby Justiciar and Hugh de Cressingham Treasurer. To Robert Bruce, who had supported his campaign against Balliol in the hope that his own claim to the throne of Scotland would be recognised and now ventured to express this hope, Edward retorted bluntly—"Do you think we have nothing to do but to win kingdoms for you?" Scotland was henceforth to be an integral part of England and it was significant that Edward did not add the title of King of Scotland to his royal style but allowed it to be tacitly included in his general title of King of England, Lord of Ireland and Duke of Aquitaine. Satisfied that the power of the Scots for further resistance had been broken and relying upon the ability of his ministers to prevent any recrudescence of trouble, Edward felt free to turn his attention again to the French war and recrossed the Tweed into England on 17 September 1296.

# Chapter Seven

# Troubles at home and abroad

Relieved of the burden of the Scottish trouble, Edward felt himself free to deal with France. The Gascon expedition had only been a temporary defensive measure and had met with little success; it had indeed done little more than act as a concrete assertion of the English claim to the Duchy. It was Edward's intention to press that claim by taking action against the French on their eastern borders; he would in this way not only avoid devastating his own province, as would be inevitable if he waged war on a large scale within its borders, but he would also be able to bring against his enemy the allied forces of a number of impecunious but warlike lords, from Adolf of Nassau, King of the Romans, to the Dukes and Counts of the Low Countries. The first and most pressing need was money, and to obtain this the king summoned a parliament at Bury St. Edmunds in November 1296. The presence at this parliament of the Scottish barons was a substantial evidence of Edward's power and success in the immediate past, pointing to the probable success of his future schemes and the danger of resisting them. The lay representatives, therefore, had little hesitation in granting liberal subsidies of a twelfth from the counties and an eighth from the boroughs. But to the demand of a fifth from the clergy Archbishop Winchelsey replied that by the recent Bull of Pope Boniface, known from its opening words as *Clericis Laicos*, they were forbidden to pay taxes to laymen without special leave. The king bade them reconsider their reply, giving them till 13 January for that purpose, and added a grim warning of the danger of persisting in a refusal. Meanwhile he despatched emissaries to negotiate for a truce with France and also took steps to consolidate his alliances on the Continent. One of the most important of these measures was the marriage of his daughter Elizabeth to the young Count John of Holland, whose father, Count Florence, had been murdered in August 1296, most opportunely for Edward's designs. John had been betrothed to Elizabeth for the past ten years, most of which time he had spent at the English court, and they were now married, on 7 January 1297, at Ipswich, where the court had been spending Christmas. The young bridegroom hastened off from Harwich some ten days after his marriage to take over the government of his country; his bride remained for the time with her father, but her sister Margaret Duchess of Brabant crossed with the Count of Holland and re-joined her husband in Brussels.

The marriage, though it had not increased Edward's popularity locally, owing to the provisions for the accompanying festivities having been commandeered without payment, strengthened his continental position. Brabant, Bar and Holland were now bound to him by marriage ties and on the day after this last wedding he renewed the treaty for the marriage of his son Edward to Philippa, daughter of the Count of Flanders, with the new proviso that if Philippa should not be available, owing either to her death or to her detention by the French king, in whose hands she was at this time, that then Edward should marry her sister Isabel. At the same time King Edward intervened to settle certain disputes between his various allies. After seeing his son-in-law off from Harwich Edward paid a visit to his favourite shrine of Walsingham, where, on 2 February, he offered to the Virgin a gold brooch set with a cameo, which had formed part of the Scottish treasure taken at Edinburgh. Thence he proceeded to Ely and on 12 February leaving Ely on his way to St. Albans he halted at the little chapel of Harrimer, the fortunate possessor of the shoes of St. Thomas of Canterbury, and while paying his respects to these relics was overtaken by a messenger with good news from France and Spain. What this good news may have been is not a matter of great importance, but it could hardly have been more than a week later that he received the news of a disaster in Gascony which more than outweighed it. On 30 January 1297 the English forces under the Earl of Lincoln and Sir John St. John, on their way to relieve Bellegarde, a fortress whose construction King Edward had supervised on the occasion of his last visit to Gascony, were surprised at night by the Count of Artois. The earl, with the rearguard, managed to escape in the darkness but St. John and eleven other knights were captured and the English army reduced practically to impotence.

The date of this disastrous defeat, 30 January, was noted by the clerical and monastic chroniclers of the time as coinciding significantly with the culmination of the king's oppression of the clergy. After a week's deliberation the clergy had come to their original conclusion that they could not grant a subsidy to the king without special leave from the Pope. This decision was reported to the king at Castle Acre; to the accompanying suggestion that he should allow them to consult the Pope he retorted that he intended to have their money whether the Pope liked it or not and that if they would not take their share in the support and defence of the realm they should not have the support and defence of the law. Accordingly on 30 January the clergy were declared to be outlawed: whatever injury or robbery were done them they would have no redress in the courts. Twelve days later all lay fees held by clerics were seized and early in March they were warned that if they remained contumacious after Easter, 14 April, their ecclesiastical fees also and all other possessions would be seized in the same way. The decrees of outlawry and forfeiture were no empty threats; they were rigidly executed; at Canterbury the sheriff's men entered the cathedral priory and fastened up the barns and larders and kitchens without giving the monks time even to take their food off the fires. The archbishop himself was reduced to living on the charity of his neighbours and his horses were taken forcibly from him while he was actually on his way to the king. The experience of the archbishop was that of many of his clergy, who were flung off their horses and saw them ridden off without hope of recovery. Occasionally the would-be robber was disappointed of his prey, as in the case of a stout Kentish parson who was riding on his best horse when he met a knight mounted on a sorry steed; to the knight's haughty demand, in the king's name, to change steeds the parson replied by so vigorous an onslaught that the knight was left half dead in the road; nor did he gain anything by complaining to the king, who bluntly retorted that "he is more stupid than a fool, who knowingly attacks one stronger than himself". But if rare individuals managed to look after themselves the position of the clergy generally was intolerable. The intrepid primate's excommunication of those who injured the clergy was countered by a threat of imprisonment for any who dared to publish the decree of excommunication; many of the clergy, especially those of the northern province, were already compromising by paying the fifth of their revenues to the king, not as a subsidy but to gain his protection and the restoration of their legal rights, and at a Synod held at St. Paul's at the end of March Archbishop Winchelsey so far relented as to allow those who chose to do so to adopt this compromise, though he himself could not reconcile his conscience to the evasion. With the exception of Oliver Sutton, Bishop of Lincoln, the archbishop was almost alone in his attitude and by Easter practically all the clergy had paid their fifth and

I

been received again into the king's favour. Having got his money and taught the clergy a sharp lesson, Edward, who could respect a good adversary and was above petty spitefulness, made his peace with Winchelsey and restored him his lands in July, the more readily because he had by that time become involved in a serious quarrel with a large section of his baronage.

On receipt of the news of the disaster at Bellegarde Edward had decided to send a strong expeditionary force to Gascony while he himself acted with his continental allies through Flanders. This plan of campaign he unfolded to an assembly of the barons at Salisbury on 24 February 1297. There was no enthusiasm for the project, which was bound to be costly and showed little prospect of being profitable, so all began to make excuses for not volunteering. Exasperated at the thwarting of his plans Edward burst out into threats, vowing to seize the lands of those who would not go and give them to those who were more complacent. The only effect of his threats was to stiffen the opposition and when the king appealed to Roger Bigod, Earl of Norfolk, to go to Gascony in his capacity of Marshal the earl replied that he would willingly go with the king and lead his host as in duty bound but that he was neither bound to go without him nor would he go. "By God, Earl," exclaimed Edward, "thou shalt either go or hang." "By that same oath, Sir King," was the reply, "I will neither go nor hang." The meeting broke up in confusion and the Earl Marshal, with the Earl of Hereford, Constable of England, constituting themselves leaders of the disaffected party, assembled formidable forces and remained upon the defensive in their estates, preventing the royal officials from levying money or supplies but not taking measures of active aggression. Edward retired from the stormy meeting at Salisbury to the more congenial atmosphere of Clarendon and the New Forest, but he did not abandon or neglect his schemes for war with France and on 16

March he wrote from Sopley offering the hand of his daughter Joan, the widowed Countess of Gloucester, to Count Amadeo of Savoy. The count was a close friend of the king's and had often acted as his ambassador on missions of importance, but the proposed strengthening of their alliance by this marriage was not destined to be achieved, for Joan now revealed the fact that she had already bestowed her hand secretly upon Ralph de Monthermer, a young squire of her husband's who had only lately been knighted. Edward's anger was extreme; he threw Monthermer into prison in Bristol Castle and deprived Joan of her estates, but the mischief was done and the marriage could not be annulled, so the proposed match with the Count of Savoy had to be abandoned.

In no very amiable frame of mind Edward made his way into the western counties, spending the greater part of April at Plympton. While here it would seem that he sent a small reinforcement to the Earl of Lincoln in Gascony, but in view of the opposition with which he had met he abandoned his original scheme for sending a large force to those parts and concentrated his efforts on preparations for his expedition to Flanders. Stores and provisions were being accumulated in immense quantities by the cheap but unpopular method of requisitioning them, while, in order to raise money, he seized all the wool, the staple article of England's trade and wealth, giving tallies for repayment, and in May he issued orders for a great muster of military tenants at London on 7 July. He also granted their freedom to the numerous Scottish nobles taken at Dunbar, on condition of their serving, with their retainers, in Flanders. On 17 June he reached Westminster and on the following day he offered in the Abbey the golden sceptre and crown and silver orb which constituted the regalia of Scotland, to be affixed to the shrine of St. Edward. When, on 7 July, the barons and gentry, in accordance with the summons, or rather "affectionate request", addressed to them in May, as-

sembled at London the king ordered the Earls of Norfolk
and Hereford, as Marshal and Constable, to make out the
muster rolls preparatory to sailing for Flanders. Both
earls refused to act, alleging that they had come by request
and not by summons and that therefore they were not
bound to perform this service. Moreover the summons
was not made in due form, the destination of the force
not being mentioned, while if it were true that the king
was going to Flanders it was questionable if service was
due, as it had never been performed there before. In anger
Edward relieved the earls of their offices, appointing
Thomas de Berkeley as Marshal and Geoffrey de Geneville
as Constable. That the quarrel did not develop into civil
war, or at least into an armed struggle between the forces
of the king and of the earls, was mainly due to the tactful
intervention of the Bishop of Durham. Finding himself
at variance with his barons and unpopular, owing to the
burden of taxation which he had imposed and his arbitrary
seizure of wool and provisions, with the merchants and
populace generally, Edward determined to make friends
with the clergy. Accordingly on 11 July he ordered the
restoration of the temporalities of Canterbury to Archbishop Winchelsey and three days later was publicly reconciled to the primate. The performance took place on a
raised stage outside Westminster Hall in full view of the
crowd, for whose edification the king made an affecting
speech, acknowledging that he had not ruled as he ought
to have and that he had made great demands upon his
subjects, but asserting that he had acted for the good of
the realm and had exacted money not for his own purposes but for the defence of his people against enemies
who thirsted for their blood. Continuing in the same
strain, he announced that he was now going across the
sea to risk his life on their behalf and begged that if he
returned safely they would receive him with goodwill or
if he did not return that they would be faithful to his son.
Finally, he begged for their prayers. The archbishop was

moved to tears, such of the barons as were present pressed forward to do homage to young Prince Edward and the emotional crowd cheered themselves hoarse. Many gave vent to their feelings in public prayers for the king, but there were not a few who concealed their feelings with private curses, and it is probable that the curses were more numerous than the prayers when the king calmly went on to ask for further subsidies. Archbishop Winchelsey was so far accommodating as to summon a convocation of the clergy to discuss the question but when they met, in August, they declined to do more than write to the Pope for leave to make a grant. The laity were even less complaisant and bluntly refused to make any grant unless the practice of taking excessive tallages and prises was abandoned and Magna Carta and the Forest Charter confirmed; they also protested against being compelled to serve abroad and expressed the opinion that the king ought not to leave England while Scotland was in the disturbed and rebellious state in which it had been since the beginning of the year.

Edward was determined to go to Flanders and the Scottish argument lost some of its force by the arrival of news of a crushing defeat inflicted on the insurgents at Irvine on 7 July, but he was compelled to concede the point that no one could be forced to serve abroad and to be content with the service of those who were willing to come for pay. The confirmation of the charters he agreed to reluctantly and finding that in spite of this the barons demurred to granting any subsidy he calmly called together a casual assembly of gentry and obtained from them a grant, which they had no power to make, of an eighth from the counties and a fifth from the boroughs. On 28 July the king appears to have paid a flying visit to St. Albans for the purpose of meeting the representatives of the barons and while there was persuaded to pardon Sir Ralph de Monthermer for his audacious marriage and to restore to him his countess and the lands of the earldom of Gloucester, on condition of serving in Flanders with fifty knights. Returning at once to London, Edward moved south to Udimore, close to Winchelsea, at which port his fleet was assembling. During one of the visits of inspection which he paid to Winchelsea he met with an adventure which might have put a summary end to all his schemes if his luck and his horsemanship had not been good. The town of Winchelsea, which had been rebuilt, or rather laid out anew on a fresh site, after the gradual destruction of the old town had been completed by the great storm of 1287, was surrounded on the side facing the harbour by a low earthen wall, between the wide battlements of which one could look straight down upon the road which wound up the face of the cliff. As Edward was riding along by this wall, gazing down on his ships, his horse took fright at a creaking windmill and grew restive; urged on with whip and spurs the terrified beast took a sudden leap over the wall. All beholders thought that the king must be killed, or at least severely injured, but the horse, landing fairly on the road, slid a dozen yards without falling and the king, without even dismounting, turned round and rode up to the town gate.

At Udimore the barons presented to the king their formal list of grievances, the main features of which have already been mentioned. To them Edward replied that in the absence of his council he could take no steps in such important matters, while to the clergy, who still adhered to their position that they could not make any grant without leave from the Pope, he answered that he was sorry that they should take up that attitude as he had no intention of consulting the Pope on the matter. With the utmost courtesy he craved their blessing and warned them that if they ventured to excommunicate his officials when they collected the subsidy everything they possessed would be forfeited. On Thursday 22 August 1297 King Edward went on board the cog "Edward", where the Chancellor, John de Langton, took leave of him and surrendered the Great Seal into his hands. On that same day the Earl Marshal and the Earl of Hereford with Sir Alan la Zouche, Sir John de Segrave and other knights, came into the Exchequer, recited the grievances which they had already laid before the king and ordered that the subsidy of an eighth and the prise of wool, which had not been granted by any recognised parliament, should not be proceeded with. The officials at once wrote an account of the occurrence and despatched it at noon the same day by special messenger. It reached Winchelsea the next day before the king had sailed and he replied promptly, insisting that the eighth should be levied, but adding that it should not be regarded as a precedent, while the prise of wool was to be made by payment and not by seizure. On the following day, while at sea, he sent back word to the regent, Prince Edward, who was then at Robertsbridge on his way to Tonbridge, confirming his previous message and adding that the Chancellor should be empowered to draw up special letters patent of protection ensuring that the subsidy should not be used as a precedent to the prejudice of those who paid it, which letters he should grant to those who were willing to pay for them. The English fleet, of some 350 ships, reached Sluys on or about 27 August and Edward at once moved up to Aardenburg, but his arrival in Flanders was marked by an event of ill omen for the success of his expedition. His fleet was composed of ships collected from all parts of the English coast, the two main factors, or factions, being the ships of the Cinque Ports and those of the Yarmouth district; between Yarmouth and the Ports jealousy and ill-feeling had been traditional for generations and a street brawl now led to an attack in force by the Portsmen on their rivals, in which thirty-two ships, including several of the largest, were burnt and some two hundred men killed. Even King Edward was not in a position to take severe measures against the hardy, independent seamen and beyond holding enquiries and making awards which were disregarded by both parties, nothing was done. Meanwhile King Edward had hastened to Bruges, where he was welcomed by the Count of Flanders with every appearance of cordiality, though the impression created by the English army with its paucity of nobles, its lack of cavalry and the predominance of wild Welsh and Irish infantry was far from favourable. The French, with superior forces, were close at hand and the citizens of Bruges had already come to terms with them and were disinclined to change their attitude to please either Edward or the Count. It was therefore decided to fall back on Ghent, and here, accordingly, for the next six months the army for whose despatch the king had estranged his subjects and endangered his crown lay idly watching their opponents, who in their turn, having a wholesome respect for the archery of the uncouth bare-legged Welsh bowmen, made no attempt to attack. After a month's inactivity, a short truce was signed on 9 October and on 23 November it was renewed to last till Lent 1298 and was then again extended till Epiphany 1299. In the meantime arrangements were made between Edward and Philip to obtain a more lasting peace through the intermediation of Pope Boniface, who was anxious to reconcile the rivals and unite them in that crusade for the recovery of the Holy Land which, with strange infatuation, he still believed possible. King Philip, however, having no intention of surrendering Gascony or of conceding more than was absolutely necessary, declined to risk a papal decision supported by the apostolic thunders of excommunication and interdict, and would only accept the arbitration of the Pope in his personal and private capacity as Benedetto Gaetani. To this Pope Boniface, seeing no alternative, agreed and in June 1298 he gave his decision and arranged a settlement practically on the basis that each party should keep what they held at the beginning of the war, that each should make amends for the damage to the other's subjects and that King Edward should marry Philip's sister Margaret, while the young Prince Edward should be betrothed to the French king's daughter Isabel—the prince's betrothal to Philippa of Flanders being annulled. To the protest of the English ambassadors that he had not ordered the restoration of Gascony the Pope replied quite frankly that it would be perfectly useless for him to do so as the French never let go of anything which they once seized and his orders would simply be ignored.

Before the papal decision had been issued the English had left Flanders, to the great relief of their unwilling hosts. The spirit of disorder and indiscipline which had shown itself in the furious quarrel of the seamen when the expedition landed soon made itself felt in the ranks of the army. Having no fighting to keep them occupied and being paid and fed irregularly the infantry, and in particular the Welsh, got out of hand and plundered and robbed their allies. The sacking of the unfortunate town of Damme so roused Edward's wrath that he hanged a number of the ringleaders and was with some difficulty dissuaded from executing the whole of the Welsh contingent. The king's severity, however, neither deterred his ruffianly soldiers nor appeased the anger of the natives and after an attempt to shoot him had failed a general massacre of all the English was planned, in which the count's two sons were involved. On 3 February 1298 the citizens of Ghent rose in arms and murdered such English as they could catch, but the king and his followers promptly armed themselves and took the field and the Welsh, who were encamped outside the city, hearing the tumult, stormed the gate and carried fire and sword through the streets. The count tried to excuse himself to King Edward and explained that he dared not punish the people, but the king bade him at once chastise them into order or he would himself inflict such chastisement as should not be forgotten for a hundred years.

When the outbreak had subsided Edward, recognising
the injuries and oppression which the citizens had suffered
at the hands of his soldiery, deemed it both just and
politic to make them liberal amends and, leaving Ghent
on 27 February, sailed from Sluys ten days later and landed
at Sandwich on 14 March 1298.

Apart from the fact that the conclusion of a truce and
the submission of the dispute to the arbitration of Pope
Boniface had put a natural end to the inglorious Flemish
expedition, affairs at home were calling urgently for
Edward's return. The crushing blow delivered at
Dunbar, which had seemed to render Scotland helpless,
had been far less decisive than it had at first appeared.
Edward had hardly recrossed the border in September
1296 before the first mutterings of revolt were heard and
during the winter and the early spring of 1297 isolated
outbreaks occurred in the north and west with in-
creasing frequency. The officers in whose hands the
control of Scotland had been placed were not particularly
fitted for such difficult and arduous work. John de
Warenne, Earl of Surrey and Sussex, had never given
proofs of more than ordinary military ability and was
now verging on the three score years and ten which in
the Middle Ages even more than in the days of the
psalmist marked the reasonable limit of man's life. He
would gladly have been relieved of his responsibility
and his royal master shortly before sailing for Flanders
endeavoured to persuade Brian Fitz-Alan of Bedale to
accept the governorship of Scotland; but as the king
thought the moment of change a suitable opportunity
for economising by reducing the salary and the forces
at the disposal of the governor Sir Brian, quite reasonably
pointing out that it would be impossible for a comparatively poor man like himself to undertake duties
which strained the resources of the wealthy earl, declined
the office and Warenne was requested to continue at his
post until fresh arrangements could be made. William de

Ormesby, the Justiciar, seems to have performed his duty with honesty but with a harshness and severity which if not unjustified was at least injudicious, and Hugh de Cressingham, the most able and energetic of the Scottish officials, was also the most unpopular; as treasurer he inevitably incurred the odium always attaching to a tax-collector, which was aggravated by his pride and by the fact that he used his position for his own enrichment, even appropriating the money intended for the fortification of Berwick.

By May 1297 the greater part of Scotland was seething with discontent and in that month William Wallace, a member of a family of knightly rank but of no eminence, who had already gained some notoriety as a troublesome outlaw, attacked and slew the Sheriff of Lanark and nearly succeeded in capturing the Justiciar at Scone. About the same time Andrew de Moray who, with his father, had been captured at Dunbar but had since escaped, headed a rising in the district of Inverness and another rising, headed by the Bishop of Glasgow and the Steward of Scotland with the support of Robert Bruce, Earl of Carrick, and Sir William Douglas, ex-Constable of Berwick, occurred in the south-west. This last, which differed from the other outbreaks in being organised in the interests of the Bruce faction, seemed the most formidable but its leaders were disunited and on 7 July, when the insurgents came face to face with a superior English force under Henry Percy at Irvine, Sir Richard de Lundy went over in disgust to the enemy and his defection was speedily followed by the surrender of the other leaders. About the same time the Bishop of Aberdeen, with the half-hearted assistance of John Comyn, Earl of Buchan, and Sir Gartenet of Mar, was endeavouring to restore the tottering English supremacy in the north of Scotland and to suppress the insurgent bands of Moray and Wallace. Encouraged by a series of local successes and by a rumour of King Edward's death Moray and

Wallace joined hands and advanced towards Stirling. Here on 10 September they came in sight of the main English army under Earl Warenne and at once took up a very strong defensive position commanding the bridge across the Forth and protected on the flank by a bend of that river. Although the English force was nominally commanded by the aged earl it was practically under control of the Treasurer, Hugh de Cressingham, whose chief anxiety was to avoid exhausting his already depleted war chest. From motives of economy Cressingham had already dismissed the contingent under Henry Percy and now he insisted on immediate action with a view to determining the campaign by a decisive victory. Accordingly on 11 September, although valuable time had been lost by Warenne's first oversleeping and then performing the ceremony of dubbing knights, a movement was made to attack the Scots. With almost incredible folly the earl insisted upon sending his cavalry across the narrow bridge, on which they could only cross two abreast, although Sir Richard de Lundy offered to show him a ford on the enemy's flank where thirty horsemen could cross at one time. When a sufficient proportion of the English cavalry had defiled on to the east side of the river the Scots swept down upon them and seized the bridgehead. In spite of a gallant charge led by Marmaduke Thwenge the forces which had crossed were cut to pieces and those still on the Stirling side of the river were seized with panic and fled, the Earl of Surrey himself not drawing rein till he had gained the security of Berwick. Less fortunate than the earl, Cressingham was slain and the Scots in mockery flayed his unwieldy corpse and distributed portions of his skin as trophies. Stirling Castle was speedily starved into surrender, all Scotland threw off the English yoke and during the winter the Scots ravaged the border counties at their will under the leadership of Wallace, his colleague Andrew de Moray, to whose military instinct the success of the Battle of

Stirling Bridge was largely due, having received at that
battle wounds of which he died a few weeks later.

One result of the disaster at Stirling was to unite the
English in face of a common danger. Prince Edward, as
Regent, had already issued summonses for a parliament
to be held in London and when it met on 6 October, with
the Scottish news still fresh in the public ear, it was
obvious that steps must at once be taken to conciliate the
large body of malcontents, of whom the Earls of Norfolk
and Hereford were the leaders. Accordingly on 10
October 1297 the Regent confirmed Magna Carta and the
Forest Charter in the fullest possible manner, remitted
the maletote or levy of 40s. on the sack of wool and
renounced the right to exact that or any tallages, aids or
prises not specially granted or sanctioned by precedent.
The Regent's action was endorsed a month later by King
Edward at Ghent. On the strength of their victory the
parliament agreed to a grant of a ninth, the illegal eighth
having been abandoned, and the clergy, drawing a clear
distinction between grants demanded for foreign expeditions and those made voluntarily for the defence of the
realm, offered subsidies of a tenth from the province of
Canterbury and of a fifth from that of York. Early in
1298 the Scots were driven back across the Border and
the siege of Roxburgh Castle was raised but no measures
on any large scale were undertaken until after the king's
return. Landing at Sandwich on 14 March, Edward met
his council at Westminster at the end of the month and
ordered a representative parliament and military levies
to assemble at York on Whit Sunday, 25 May, and he also
issued commissions for a general enquiry as to the
oppressive actions of his officials with regard to the
taking of supplies for the Flemish expedition. During the
next four weeks he visited St. Albans and his favourite
shrines of St. Edmund's and Walsingham, arriving at
York for the Whitsun parliament. Here, at the instance of
the Earls of Norfolk and Hereford, who feared that the

king might evade the undertaking to which he had set his seal while abroad, he signified his assent to the demand for the confirmation of the Charters, the Bishop of Durham and the Earls of Surrey and Gloucester swearing on his behalf that when he returned victorious he would perform his promise.

A month later the English army, consisting mainly of cavalry, with a contingent of Welsh infantry, mustered at Roxburgh. A detachment under the Bishop of Durham was detailed to besiege Dirlton and two neighbouring castles while the main body moved on to Kirk-Liston. Owing to the prevalence of contrary winds the supplies which were to have come round by sea failed to arrive and the troops were for some days in great straits. When at last, on 19 July, provisions reached the camp an injudicious distribution of wine to the starving Welshmen resulted in their becoming drunk and attacking their English comrades; the English men-at-arms retaliated vigorously and scattered the Welsh in flight. The latter at first meditated joining the Scots but, intimidated by King Edward's calm acceptance of their desertion and his warning of the punishment that would follow, they sullenly fell in at the rear of the English army and waited to see how events would shape themselves. On 20 July, just as Edward had determined to retire on Edinburgh and form a fresh scheme of campaign the Earls of Angus and March, with Bishop Bek of Durham, came to him with a spy, who said that the Scots were only six leagues distant, at Falkirk in Selkirk Forest, intending to pursue him on his way to Edinburgh. "As God lives, who hath hitherto delivered me out of all my troubles," exclaimed the king, "they need not pursue me, for I will go and meet them this day." To the surprise of all who were not in the secret, camp was at once struck and the whole force marched off in the direction of Linlithgow, near which town they bivouacked on the moor for the night, lying with their arms by their side and their horses tethered near them. During the night the king's charger, taking fright at some noise, dragged its ropes and trampled on its sleeping master, breaking two of his ribs. An alarm was spread through the camp that the king had been injured, there were cries of treachery and all sprang to arms, but quiet was soon restored and at daybreak King Edward himself was the first to mount and lead his host through Linlithgow towards the enemy. Upon coming in sight of the Scots a brief halt was made for the celebration of mass in honour of St. Mary Magdalene, whose feast-day it was (22 July). Wallace had not selected his position with any great skill; his front was protected by a small stream and a swamp, strengthened by a rough barricade of stakes and ropes, and his forces were posted on rising ground, but the position was not particularly strong and the manner in which he disposed his troops showed no military genius and suggests that he had the abilities of a guerrilla leader rather than of a great commander. The infantry, who formed the bulk of his army, he grouped in four solid circular masses with their levelled spears projecting on all sides; between these circles, or "schiltrons", he placed his archers and in the rear his small force of cavalry. His traditional remark to his men, "I have brought you to the ring, hop [dance] if you can"* does not suggest that he had any extravagant expectations of success. Spiritually fortified by the mass which the Bishop of Durham had celebrated, Edward proposed to postpone the engagement until his men and horses had had a much needed meal, but his barons urged that the delay would be dangerous and orders were given for an immediate advance. As the Welsh infantry sullenly refused to move forward Edward opened the attack with

---

*It is probable that, like most traditional speeches, it was never made, as the expression appears to have been proverbially applied in cases where a leader had got his men into a hopeless position and then left them to get out of it by themselves. In a contemporary poem against lawyers (Wright, *Political Songs*, 339) we have: "Attourneis in cuntré theih geten silver for noht; Theih maken men biginne that they nevere hadden thought; And whan theih comen to the ring, hoppe if hii kunne."

his cavalry, which he divided into four lines, keeping one line in reserve. The first line, under the Earls of Norfolk, Hereford and Lincoln, on encountering the swamp made a wide detour to the left and had not arrived on the scene when the second line, under the Bishop of Durham, wheeling to the right, had come within striking distance. Bishop Bek, unwilling to run any needless risk, halted his men and proposed to await the arrival of the third line, led by the king himself, but Ralph Basset of Drayton, contemptuously bidding him get to his mass and not meddle with military matters, led a charge before which the Scottish cavalry crumbled and fled. Few in numbers and partly composed of men who considered themselves the social superiors of Wallace and were jealous of his position, the Scottish mounted troops, with the honourable exception of Sir John Stewart and a few others, made no resistance and abandoned the infantry to their fate. The archers were speedily ridden down and although the schiltrons with their bristling spears offered a sturdy defiance to the English cavalry they were powerless for offence and when once their serried ranks were broken by a storm of stones and arrows from the English and Welsh, who now deemed it politic to come in on the winning side, they were easily dispersed and cut to pieces. As Dunbar had been fatal to the nobility so Falkirk was fatal to the common people in whom Wallace's strength lay, and he ceased to play any prominent part in the Scottish War of Independence, shortly afterwards resigning his position as "guardian of Scotland"; on his resignation the wardenship was vested in representatives of the two chief factions, John Comyn of Badenoch and Robert Bruce, Earl of Carrick. The latter at the time of Wallace's defeat at Falkirk was at the head of a small force in the southwest. Accordingly, after resting for a couple of weeks at Stirling to recover from his injury, King Edward at the end of August struck across to Ayr, from which town

Bruce discreetly retired. Supplies again failing to come round by sea and the English army being again reduced to severe straits for lack of provisions, Edward hastily retired, ravaging Bruce's lands and seizing his castle of Lochmaben on the way, and reached Carlisle on 8 September.

The English magnates, weary of fighting in a difficult and desolate country, could not be induced to face the still greater hardships of a winter campaign and Edward was obliged to allow the greater part of them, headed by the irreconcilable Earls of Norfolk and Hereford, to return home while he himself remained in the north till the end of the year 1298.

K

# Chapter Eight

# Last Years

During January 1299 King Edward visited his favourite shrines in East Anglia and on 12 March he reached Westminster, where he met his parliament. The terms of the papal award were discussed and the proposal for the marriage of the king and his son with the French princesses was accepted, although no provision had been made for the cession of the lost Duchy of Aquitaine. The magnates cared little about these continental possessions and were certainly not prepared to risk the expense and trouble of another war with France for their recovery; for the time they were far more interested in domestic affairs, endeavouring to extort from King Edward the promised confirmation of Magna Carta and more especially of the Forest Charter. Edward aroused suspicion and anger by his endeavours to evade the fulfilment of his oaths and when he suddenly, without warning, left Westminster these feelings were intensified. The nobles who rode out after him to Harrow were not inclined to accept his excuse that he had only come there for change of air as Westminster did not suit him, but they had to be content with his promise that if they returned they should have the answer of his council next day. When the answer was at last forthcoming it proved far from satisfactory, for the king, borrowing Becket's favourite device for avoiding a definite issue, had granted their demands "saving the rights of the crown". On 3 April Edward set his seal to the delusive confirmation of the charters, at the same time ordering the promised perambulation of the forests, which was an essential part of the confirmation of the Forest Charter. Seeing that the magnates were not appeased, Edward tried to win the people to his side and caused these newly sealed proclamations to be read publicly in St. Paul's churchyard. But although the crowd were duly impressed with the royal generosity when they heard the contents of the charters, they were quick to grasp the significance of the saving clause and of the similar reservations attached to the grant of the perambulation. After a brief adjournment the parliament reassembled at Stepney in May and Edward abandoned, or explained away, the obnoxious saving clause and appointed a commission to deal with the perambulation. At the same time he despatched a mission under Count Amadeo of Savoy and the Earls of Warwick and Lincoln to France to meet the papal nuncio at Montreuil, the Count of Savoy being empowered to act as the king's proxy for the betrothal to Margaret while the Earl of Lincoln was to play a similar part between Prince Edward and Isabel.

In order to keep in touch with his envoys Edward moved down to Dover at the beginning of June, but after a couple of weeks went on pilgrimage to the shrine of St. Richard at Chichester. While on his way thither, on 21 June at Lamberhurst, he received good news from France, probably of the signing of the treaty at Montreuil two days before. From Lewes he sent his son back hastily to Canterbury, where he rejoined him on 6 July. Here on 14 July Edward received the papal nuncio, the Bishop of Vicenza, and himself confirmed the treaty. Philip, urged by the Pope, had been endeavouring to obtain favourable terms for the Scots from King Edward, though he had declined to give them anything more solid than his moral support. Edward, knowing that the French king would not imperil the peace for the sake of the Scots, would not agree to their being included in the treaty but was so far complaisant as to release the ex-king,

John Balliol, from confinement. Accordingly on 18 July 1299 Balliol was sent across from Dover to Wissant and there delivered to the Bishop of Vicenza, eventually retiring to the seclusion of his ancestral Norman estates at Bailleul. At the moment of the ex-king's embarkation at Dover his luggage was seized and opened; a quantity of money and plate found in it was returned to him but the Scottish seal and a golden coronet which he had somehow contrived to retain during the three years of his captivity were forfeited.

At the end of August, when all arrangements had been made for his marriage, Edward spent a few days hunting in Woolmer Forest, sending his son on to Canterbury to receive the nobles who were assembling there for the approaching festivities. On 9 September, while he was at Chartham, the king received news of the landing of his bride. Next day he rode into Canterbury and met Margaret and her escort, in which were numbered the Dukes of Burgundy and Brittany and a crowd of lesser nobles. Elaborate preparations had been made for the reception of the royal party; the archbishop's palace had been put at their disposal and extra accommodation provided in the shape of great tents and temporary buildings, for the adornment of which quantities of cloth had been hired from the manufacturers of Candlewick Street, the busy centre of London's weaving industry. Besides the cosmopolitan crowd of nobles and sightseers, minstrels of many nationalities were assembled and were busily employed on the morning of Friday 11 September when the marriage of the king, still upright and vigorous for all the burden of his sixty years, and the fair girlish princess was celebrated at the door of the historic cathedral by Archbishop Winchelsey. When the ceremony was over the rest of the day was spent in gaiety, tilting and other sports and games and feasting. Edward had good reason to feel pleased with the match he had made, by which he had gained not only peace with France but a wife who was beautiful and charming alike in person and character, a worthy successor to Eleanor of Castile. A week was spent at Canterbury and another at the royal castle of Leeds and then, in October, the court moved to Westminster. Here the king met his council to discuss the question of another campaign against Scotland. Although the opinion of his advisers was almost unanimously against undertaking a winter campaign Edward insisted upon ordering a muster of troops at York for 12 November. On 3 November the king bade farewell to Queen Margaret at Langley and began his journey northwards by a visit to St. Albans, where he paid his devotions to the saint and made a public appeal for the prayers of the convent. At the same time he sent offerings to Walsingham, St. Edmund's and Ely and wrote to Archbishop Winchelsey desiring general prayers to be made for his success. In spite, however, of these devout precautions he found on his arrival at York on 15 November a very modest force of cavalry, composed almost entirely of hired men-at-arms, and practically no infantry. Such foot soldiers as had been got together refused bluntly to face a winter campaign for wages which were largely paid in the debased Flemish coin which had flooded the country since Edward's alliance with Flanders. Edward gave instructions that the infantry, of whose value he was fully aware, should be treated with tact and persuaded to join by promises of vague benefits, but it was with a force far too weak for any useful purpose that he entered Berwick on 13 December. Here he kept Christmas 1299, while his queen and his son, who had spent the early part of December at St. Albans, where Queen Margaret had won the hearts of the monks by her gracious piety and devotion, were at Windsor. Away from his family, deserted by his nobles, unsupported by his people, King Edward spent a far from happy Christmas on the Border, the gloom being deepened by the news of the fall of Stirling Castle. At last the king was obliged to see that his enterprise was hopeless, that the winter season gave the Scots too great an advantage and that the only course possible was to abandon the expedition, return to England and summon another army for Whitsun. Accordingly on 1 January 1300 King Edward recrossed the Border and by the end of the month had rejoined his wife at Windsor.

The month of March was signalised by the holding of a full representative parliament at Westminster. A demand was immediately put forward by the Earl Marshal and Archbishop Winchelsey for the confirmation of the charters. For some days the king refused to give a definite answer to the demand, spending the interval in putting personal pressure upon individual barons in order to divide his opponents and create a royalist party. In this he was fairly successful, his willingness to accept the moderate subsidy of a twentieth producing a corresponding willingness on the part of the barons to modify their extreme demands. His action, however, had created, or rather increased, suspicion in the minds of the baronial leaders and when he at last agreed to confirm Magna Carta they demanded that his confirmation should be corroborated by the seals of all the bishops and earls, as guarantors of his good faith. Not unnaturally incensed at the suggestion, Edward bluntly refused, asking angrily whether they considered him a child or a traitor. Finally, on 28 March, the Great Charter and the Forest Charter were confirmed and the Archbishop was instructed to support the confirmation by declaring all those who infringed the charters excommunicate. The royal consent was also given to a series of articles amplifying the provisions of the Great Charter and dealing with the abuse of purveyance and other less important legal points. The long promised perambulation of the forests was at last taken in hand, though this concession was tempered by the appending of a clause saving the rights of the crown. At the same time steps were taken for the reform

of the currency. During Edward's expedition to Flanders
in 1297 he had found it expedient to propitiate the
Flemish merchants by allowing them to pay for English
wool with the coins known as pollards and crockards,
of base metal silvered over; a great quantity of these
base coins had thus come into circulation in England, to
the confusion and detriment of trade. In 1299 orders were
issued, and enforced by terms of imprisonment, that two
of these coins should pass for one penny sterling and now,
at the March parliament of 1300, the circulation of any
variety of this base money was entirely prohibited.
Measures were also promptly taken for the issue of a new
coinage and it is rather remarkable, in view of what we
know of the excellence of English metal-workers of the
period, that the work appears to have been entrusted
entirely to foreigners, about 150 moneyers being brought
over in April from Namur, Bruges, Brussels and Paris.

As soon as the parliament was over Edward left
Westminster, where on 21 March he had attended the
interment of his brother Edmund of Lancaster, whose
body had been brought from Gascony, where he had
died in 1296, and was now laid to rest in Westminster
Abbey in the spot marked by one of the most beautiful
monuments in the Abbey. Easter, 1300, was spent by the
court at St. Albans with much magnificence and Edward
was in his most gracious mood. Among those present
were the two officers who had been in command of
Stirling Castle the previous year, and when he had heard
from them details of the hardships which they had en-
dured before they were reduced to capitulate, the king
vowed to be revenged on the traitor Scots. The army had
been summoned to muster at Carlisle at Midsummer, and
before moving northwards Edward went as usual on
pilgrimage to his favourite shrines. The queen, who was
not in a condition to undertake rapid journeys, did not
accompany her husband but went by gradual stages
towards York. At the little village of Brotherton on the

Wharfe she was delivered of a son, who was at once given the name of Thomas, on 1 June. King Edward was at Selby Abbey when he received the news the same day and he at once paid a flying visit to Brotherton and sent offerings to the child's name saints, St. Thomas Becket at Canterbury and St. Thomas Cantelupe at Hereford, for whose formal canonisation the king made several appeals to different popes. Young Thomas of Brotherton is recorded to have displayed a proper patriotism at a remarkably early age by rejecting the attentions and milk of the French nurse who was first provided for him and only allowing himself to be pacified and fed by a nurse of English origin.

Reaching Carlisle at Midsummer, 1300, as arranged, the king found an army assembled but weak in numbers and poor in quality. Crossing into Galloway at the beginning of July the English forces found themselves in a desolate and difficult country, rendered the more dangerous and inhospitable by the rainy weather. No enemy was visible and no plunder; the Scots and their castles alike were safely hidden behind the swollen swamps and bogs. The castle of Caerlaverock resisted for a week but its fall was an event of no military significance and would hardly have deserved notice had it not been that some rhyming herald (possibly "le Roy Robert" or "le Roy Capenny", two of the contemporary Kings at Arms) made it the occasion for a lengthy poem containing an elaborate blazon of the arms of the English nobles there present. While Edward was at Kirkcudbright, where he fixed his headquarters for the last half of July, after the fall of Caerlaverock, Archbishop Winchelsey arrived at Carlisle bearing a letter from the Pope. The letter in question had been written as long previously as 27 June 1299 under the influence of the Scottish envoys to the papal court and set forward the astounding claim that Scotland was a fief of Rome, and that the disposal of the crown belonged to the Pope, with the natural corollary that Edward must cease from oppressing the Scots and submit any claim that he wished to make to the Scottish throne to the consideration of the Pope. Why the letter had not been delivered before is not clear but it is at least possible that Winchelsey had wisely withheld it and addressed a private remonstrance to the Pope and that Pope Boniface had let the matter drop until the Scots had strengthened their appeal with substantial gifts. Such a reminder, coming in the year 1300 when the centennial Jubilee made Rome more than ever the centre of Christendom, appealed to the vanity and ambition of Boniface and caused him to order the delivery of the letter. Whatever Winchelsey's feelings may have been he was too devoted a son of the Church to refuse obedience and accordingly set forth in pursuit of Edward. At Carlisle the archbishop was held up for some weeks, unable to obtain an escort or a safe-conduct that would enable him to pass through Galloway, which was swarming with wild Scots. With much difficulty he got a message taken round by sea to the king and received a reply politely regretting that there was no safe way for him to come and suggesting that he should join the queen in Yorkshire and await the king's return. Winchelsey, however, was a man of spirit and, hearing that Edward had returned to the neighbourhood of Caerlaverock and was at Sweetheart Abbey, he braved the quicksands and morasses at the head of Solway Firth and reached the royal headquarters about 25 August. The king was at dinner when he arrived but gave him an audience next day. When the papal letter had been read in Latin and French Edward replied that in a matter touching the rights of the crown it was the custom for the Council to be consulted before any answer could be given and that he would lay it before them at a convenient date. With this the archbishop was dismissed and a few days later Edward disbanded his army and took up his quarters at the Abbey of Holmcultram, where he was joined by Queen Margaret. The expedition had been practically barren of results, the infantry had deserted almost in a body and such troops as had remained with the king had had little to do, the Scots leaving the rain and the barren poverty of the land to fight for them and avoiding pitched battles. Several efforts had been made by the Scots to obtain terms from Edward but he had rejected their overtures contemptuously; now, however, faced with disaffection in his ranks and under pressure from the Pope and the King of France he was forced to abandon the idea of another campaign and on 30 October he signed a truce, to last until Whitsun (21 May) 1301, at Dumfries. Shortly afterwards he returned to Carlisle and in the middle of December reached Northampton, where he spent Christmas.

During the last ten days of January 1301 a parliament sat at Lincoln which was remarkable in several respects. Like that held the previous spring it was fully representative and, so far as possible, it was composed of the same persons who had sat in the parliament of 1300, of which it was in a sense a continuation or adjournment. The chief business of the earlier parliament had been to obtain an order for the perambulation of the forests and the results of that perambulation had now to be considered. To the demand that the perambulation should be completed in those parts which had not yet been dealt with and that effect should be given to the decisions of the perambulating justices by the disafforesting of the districts affected the king would not give a direct answer but, falling back upon a legal quibble, declared that the disafforestments should be made if the parliament could assure him that he would not thereby infringe his coronation oath to maintain the rights of the crown. Not unnaturally they declined to accept the responsibility and replied that it would be more becoming for him to keep his recent oath and do justice to his subjects. At the same time they presented a Bill of twelve articles, repeating their demands for the confirmation of the two charters, the immediate and thorough execution of their provisions and the annulment of acts contrary thereto, the abolition of illegal purveyances, and other reforms; if these conditions were granted they expressed their willingness to make a grant of a fifteenth in place of the twentieth previously voted, though they took the opportunity to reaffirm the archbishop's contention that the goods of the clergy should not be taxed without special licence from the Pope. To all these articles the king signified his assent, with the exception of the last. It is generally stated that the Bill was submitted to the king on behalf of the parliament by Henry de Keighley, knight of the shire for Lancashire, and that Edward was so angered by what he considered the outrageous nature of these demands that he threw the knight into prison. The incident is rather obscure but it seems fairly clear that Keighley did not act publicly as the "first Speaker of the Commons", as he has been termed, but was the secret intermediary by whom the offensive petition was delivered into the king's hands, as it was not until three months later that King Edward was able to discover his identity and obtain his arrest. It is also clear that the king's anger was not stirred by the twelve articles, the novelty of which had long worn off, but by something much more personal and unexpected. This was nothing less than a demand that the Treasurer, Walter de Langton, Bishop of Coventry and Lichfield, his most intimate minister, should be removed and that appointments to the offices of Chancellor, Treasurer and Chief Justice should be made subject to the approval of the kingdom, that is to say of parliament. Edward was not the man to submit to such dictation; as he pertinently pointed out every noble, even every head of a family, appointed and discharged his own servants and would resent the interference of an outsider, and he had no intention of being refused a privilege which all his subjects exercised or of being a king in name and nothing more. If they had any grievance against his ministers, let them state it, but neither Justice, Treasurer nor Chancellor should be appointed save at his own pleasure. No more was heard of the proposal for this extraordinary extension of popular control, but the attacks on the Treasurer, instigated by Winchelsey, were renewed a year later when Sir John de Lovetot accused him of infringements of most of the Ten Commandments and of a few other offences, such as simony, which had been overlooked by the compilers of the Decalogue. As a result Langton was suspended and compelled to pay a visit to the papal court, where, after he had been well fleeced, his innocence was established in June 1303. By way of showing his own zeal for the good governance of the Church the Pope at the same time authorised the slandered Treasurer to bestow benefices upon two of his nephews who had reached the mature ages of ten and twelve years respectively.

The representatives of the shires were dismissed and the Lincoln parliament dissolved on 30 January, but the magnates remained in council to consider what reply should be made to the letter of Pope Boniface claiming the disposal of the realm of Scotland. At last on 12 February a letter was drawn up in the name of the whole baronage asserting that there was no precedent for an English king answering for the temporal rights of the crown to any judge, ecclesiastical or secular, that such an act would be derogatory to the crown and that if the king ever contemplated such a step it would be their duty to prevent it. They also added that the Church of Rome had never had any temporal rights over Scotland, of which the overlordship notoriously belonged to the English king. To this letter, which was executed as usual in duplicate, were attached the seals of seven earls and nearly a hundred lesser lords, representing not only the barons actually present at Lincoln but also others whose assents and seals were added later. It would seem, however, that the letter was never sent and it is even doubtful whether King Edward's own reply, which was to the same effect but more politely enwrapped in a shroud of verbiage and decorated with historical assertions even wilder than those of the Pope, was actually despatched. However this may be, the papal claim was quite definitely rejected and preparations were made for a further Scottish campaign in the summer of 1301.

While at Lincoln King Edward bestowed upon his son, Edward of Carnarvon, the principality of Wales, which has ever since been regarded as the peculiar possession of the eldest son of the reigning sovereign. The revival of the title Prince of Wales gave some satisfaction to the Welsh people, who were also able to feel that if their prince was not of the ancient line or of Welsh descent he was at least born in Wales. The Prince, now at the end of his seventeenth year, had been with his father on the last Scottish campaign and had on several occasions acted as his father's representative but seems already to have been showing signs of the frivolous and unworthy character which distinguished him in later life, and the evidence of these characteristics accumulates rapidly during the next few years even before they are exposed to the fierce light that beats upon a throne. During the three or four months that intervened between the termination of the Lincoln parliament and council and the beginning of the new Scottish expedition Edward was unusually restful. The last week of March was spent at Evesham, the first half of April at Feckenham and, with the exception of a short visit to Hereford, probably on pilgrimage to the shrine of Thomas Cantelupe, the king remained in Worcestershire till the middle of May, when he moved on to Kenilworth. Here he spent another two weeks in the company of his family, including the little Thomas of Brotherton, whom he had ordered to be brought from Northampton, and his daughter Elizabeth, whose husband the Count of Holland had died on 10

November 1299. It is not, perhaps, reading too much significance into the contrast between these quiet weeks and the restless progresses of his earlier years if we conclude that age was beginning to tell upon the strenuous monarch and that he found the need for recruiting his strength before starting on a fresh campaign which he foresaw might be lengthy and intended should be decisive. At the beginning of June the court broke up, Queen Margaret going to Woodstock, where on 5 August she gave birth to a second son, Edmund, while the king and the Prince of Wales made their way to the Border. The prince with the Welsh infantry and a small force of cavalry was to enter Scotland from Carlisle on the west, while King Edward with the main army was to operate from Berwick on the east. Edward accordingly crossed to Coldstream on 20 July and moved westwards to Peebles where he fixed his headquarters during the early part of August, afterwards moving to Lanark and Glasgow. Most of September was spent at Bothwell and October at Dunipace, from which place he paid frequent visits to Linlithgow, where he was building a peel or castle. This seems to have been completed, or at least well advanced, by the end of the month as he spent the whole of November, December and January 1302 at Linlithgow and was there joined by the queen for Christmas. Of fighting we hear nothing, the Scots under John Comyn again pursuing Fabian tactics, but the royal forces were steadily reduced by the desertion of the infantry and the death of many horses from the inclemency of the winter, so that when the Abbot of Compiègne arrived as envoy from King Philip, once more urging his royal brother-in-law to grant a truce to the Scots, Edward was not unwilling to listen to him. At the end of December the patriot Bishop of St. Andrews returned from France under a safe-conduct and on 26 January a truce was signed to last until 30 November (St. Andrew's Day) 1302. The forces under the Prince of Wales were recalled to Linlithgow and, after visiting Edinburgh and Roxburgh, Edward returned to England on 19 February 1302.

The truce with Scotland formed part of a treaty with France by which the existing truce between France and England was extended to the same date, St. Andrew's Day, though Edward expressly declined to admit that the Scots were allies of the French or to acknowledge the right of John de Balliol to be termed king. Philip was now anxious to be on good terms with England as he was fully occupied with other quarrels. The claims of Pope Boniface VIII to temporal power as well as to ecclesiastical supremacy had brought him into violent collision with Philip IV, who intended to be paramount on the Continent and was quite prepared, if necessary, to oppose the weight of his sword to the shadowy claims of papal autocracy. The immediate result was that Boniface made a bid for Edward's support, sending the Bishop of Spoleto to England as his envoy, and abandoned not only his claim to dispose of the Scottish throne but also his support of the Scots, whom he now treated as rebels against Edward's just authority. Edward, however, was not disposed to ally himself with Rome and saw greater prospects of profit in remaining neutral. In March 1302 the burghers of Bruges had risen in fury against their oppressors and massacred all the French upon whom they could lay hands. Their example had been followed by other Flemish cities and when King Philip had sent a great army to execute vengeance upon them the despised burghers had inflicted a crushing defeat on the chivalry of France at Courtrai in July, slaying the Count of Artois and many other nobles and men of high rank. A parliament was sitting at Westminster when the news of this disaster to the French reached England and the establishment of peace on a more permanent footing was under discussion. A suggestion that Edward should go in person to visit the French king was eventually rejected but negotiations continued. The Flemings were at the same time pressing King Edward to come to their assistance; unwilling either to break with France or to see Flanders crushed Edward contrived to make Queen Margaret believe that a plot had been formed by some of the French nobles to betray King Philip to his enemies. She at once sent word of warning to her brother and the fear of such treachery played a considerable part in inducing him to abandon the siege of Douai and withdraw from Flanders early in October. In the same month of October Queen Margaret's other brother, Sir Louis of France, came to Westminster, where parliament was again sitting, and further negotiations resulted in the prolongation of the truce from 30 November 1302 to Easter 1303. The renewal of the truce was signed at Amiens on 26 November, only four days before the original date of its termination and information of its renewal not having reached Bordeaux by the end of the month the citizens of that town gladly availed themselves of the expiration of the truce to eject the French garrison and declare for England, their example being followed by other places in Gascony. Philip was not in a position to recover his hold on Gascony and, after a further prolongation of the truce to Whitsun 1303, a definite treaty of alliance between France and England was executed at Paris on 20 May 1303 and subsequently ratified on 10 July by Edward, who was then at Perth. By this treaty Aquitaine was restored to the English crown, the Prince of Wales performing homage for the Duchy as his father's representative, and a peace was established between the two countries which remained unbroken until the end of Edward's reign.

In November 1302 Edward's daughter Elizabeth, Countess of Holland, was married to Humphrey de Bohun, Earl of Hereford and Essex, son of the earl who had carried on a little war with his neighbour in the Welsh March, the Earl of Gloucester, and had afterwards,

Conway Castle

Edward I

as Constable, joined with the Earl Marshal in leading the baronial opposition to the king. The contrarious Constable had died in 1298 and by the settlement of the Bohun estates on the issue of Humphrey and Elizabeth his titles and wide lands were brought into the circle of the royal family. In the case of his comrade Roger Bigod, Earl of Norfolk and Marshal, Edward's triumph was more complete and more personal. The childless earl, having quarrelled with his brother and heir and fearing the weight of the king's displeasure now that he stood alone, contrived to gain the royal favour and to disinherit his brother in April 1302 by resigning all his lands and honours to King Edward in return for an annuity of £1,000. Upon his death in 1306 the earldom of Norfolk lapsed to the crown and was at once bestowed by Edward upon his little son Thomas of Brotherton. The death of the king's cousin Edmund Earl of Cornwall in October 1300 had brought that exceptionally valuable earldom into Edward's hands and the marriage of his nephew Thomas, already Earl of Lancaster, Derby and Leicester, with the daughter and heiress of Henry de Lacy, Earl of Lincoln and Salisbury ensured the union of five earldoms. Gloucester was already held by the king's grandson and young John de Warenne, heir to the aged Earl of Surrey and Sussex, had probably already been marked down as a suitable husband for the king's granddaughter, Joan de Barre, whose hand was bestowed upon him in 1306, after his accession to the joint earldom. Practically the whole of the territorial nobility had thus been brought within the royal circle by the end of Edward's reign.

As soon as the truce with Scotland had expired Edward began to make preparations for a fresh expedition and in January 1303 he sent orders to a number of northern barons to join John de Segrave, his lieutenant in Scotland, and take action against the Scots preparatory to his own advent. Segrave's forces, divided into three sections, were

L

in the neighbourhood of Roslyn on 23 February when the
Scots under John Comyn of Badenoch and Simon
Fraser suddenly fell upon the main division early in the
morning. No proper watch was being kept, the English
were taken completely by surprise and Segrave and a
number of other knights were captured. The paymaster,
Ralph de Manton, against whom Simon Fraser had an old
grudge for wages unpaid, was executed and although
Segrave and some of the other prisoners were rescued by
an attack by the division under Robert Nevill the loss in
men and prestige was serious. By the middle of May
Edward was once more on the Border. As in the case of
his last expedition, he sent a force under the Prince of
Wales and the Earl of Ulster into Galloway while he
himself acted on the east, entering Roxburgh on Ascen-
sion Day, 16 May 1303. Here he spent two weeks and
then moved up to Perth, which was his headquarters
during June and July. The first half of August was
devoted to the siege of the castle of Brechin, which only
fell when its gallant commander, Sir Thomas Maule, was
slain by a shot from one of the English mangonels.
Edward then advanced north as far as Aberdeen, Banff
and Elgin and while at Lochindorb about the end of
September received the submission of the greater number
of the northern magnates and gentry and the surrender
of their castles, in which he placed his own garrisons. He
then moved slowly down to Dunfermline, where he
spent November and the following three months. Of
the western army we know practically nothing beyond
the fact that the country through which it passed was
systematically wasted and that it was at Linlithgow by the
end of September, when the Irish infantry, finding themselves unpaid, unfed and unable to obtain redress, were
preparing to desert in a body. The Prince of Wales
established himself at Perth for the Christmas season and
early in 1304 was entrusted by his father with the conduct
of the negotiations with John Comyn of Badenoch and

the other Scottish leaders. Liberal terms were granted
and on 16 February Comyn and most of the other leaders
did homage to King Edward and made their peace with
him by submitting to short periods of banishment and
fines, estimated at three years' value of their estates.
William Wallace and Sir Simon Fraser almost alone remained at large and were declared outlaws, a reward of
£100 being offered for the capture of Wallace. At the
beginning of March 1304 the court left Dunfermline,
burning the spacious buildings of the Abbey on the grounds
that they had formerly been used for Scottish parliaments,
and moved to St. Andrews, where a joint parliament of
the English and Scots was held to consider the settlement
of Scotland. From Caithness to Galloway there was not a
fortress or stronghold of any importance that still held
out with the notable exception of Stirling Castle. On 2
March the king had written to the Earl of March and
Dunbar urging him to act more energetically in the
Stirling district, expressing surprise at his slackness and
delay and applying to him the current proverbial rhyme
of the warrior who only found his sword when the
campaign was over:

> "Quant la guerre fu finee
> Si troft Audegier s'espee."

Now, at the end of April Edward himself took control of
the operations and laid siege to the castle. All the resources of military engineering were brought to bear upon
the fortress; a dozen great engines for casting stone balls
weighing as much as three hundredweight apiece, scores
of lesser machines for throwing stones, bolts and flaming
missiles, wooden towers to enable the besiegers to shoot
over the walls, and battering rams were employed. On
the other side the defenders had the advantage of an
exceptionally strong position on a dominant rock; when
some of their stores had been destroyed by fire they
placed the remainder in safety in caves hollowed out of

the solid rock; they were well supplied with provisions
and munitions and kept up a continual fire upon their
assailants. On several occasions King Edward, who
persisted in exposing himself to danger in spite of the
remonstrances of his attendants, had narrow escapes. Once
a bolt from a crossbow grazed the light armour that he
was wearing and stuck in his saddlebow; drawing it out
he spat on it and shaking it towards the castle walls
vowed to hang the man who shot it. On another occasion a huge stone hurled from one of the castle engines
crashed down and would have struck him to the ground
if his horse had not suddenly reared. At last provisions
began to run short in the castle, the moat had been filled
up and although one ram had broken itself unavailingly
against the stout walls a second of less elaborate but more
effective construction had made a breach. The gallant
constable of the castle, Sir William Oliphant, seeing that
further resistance was hopeless offered to capitulate on
terms but Edward would not hear of anything short of
unconditional surrender and on 24 July Oliphant and
his comrades surrendered the castle and submitted themselves to the king's mercy with the picturesque and
theatrical display of humility and penitence customary on
such occasions. Edward, after a proper display of indignation and threats, sent them all off to honourable confinement in various English castles, only exacting the death
penalty from an English deserter who had betrayed the
castle to the Scots.

While the fall of Stirling completed the military
operations and put a seal to the conquest of Scotland it
was not until just a month later, on 25 August, that
Edward recrossed the Border, leaving Aymer de Valence
in charge of Scotland. At the end of October he reached
the royal manor of Burstwick and here he spent seven
weeks resting from the fatigues of the past eighteen
months. Christmas 1304 was spent at Lincoln with much
magnificence and general rejoicing. Edward had indeed

a right to feel satisfied. Relations with France were better than they had been at any time during his reign and the Duchy of Aquitaine had been recovered without the expenditure of blood or money. Scotland had been crushed, not stunned by a single sudden blow from which she would soon recover but worn down by unwearying and deliberate campaigning. So sure was Edward of his triumph that he could act with generosity towards the conquered Scots and many of his most resolute opponents were placed in positions of honour and responsibility, to hold for him the very castles and shires which they had recently endeavoured to hold against him; and another sign that marked his conviction that the settlement of Scotland was accomplished was the return of the courts of King's Bench and Exchequer in December 1304 to London from York, where they had been established for just over seven years. At home the baronial opposition had been deprived of leaders by the death of Bohun, the muzzling of Bigod and the absorption of the great territorial lordships into the royal circle. The clergy were equally impotent. The quarrel of Pope Boniface with Philip of France had compelled him to seek Edward's support and to abandon his faithful servant Archbishop Winchelsey; the archbishop had been actually under sentence of excommunication for six months from the autumn of 1301 for his courageous endeavour to prevent the alien pluralist Theobald de Bar, half-brother of Count Henry, from holding that same wealthy benefice of Pagham which had been the spark to kindle the explosion between Becket and Henry II. Winchelsey's enemy the Treasurer Langton had emerged triumphant from the attacks upon him, and the humiliation of Pope Boniface at the hands of Sciarra Colonna and other enemies, resulting in his death at the end of 1303, had deprived the Church of her most vigorous champion and marked the beginning of the temporary eclipse of Roman supremacy. Unfortunately, however, the constant preoccupation of the king, his ministers and lords with Scotland and the absence of the courts from London had inevitably resulted in an increase of lawlessness in England, which had been augmented by poverty, due to heavy taxation and light harvests, and the release of large numbers of felons, who obtained their liberty on condition of serving in the army, from which they often deserted or were, at any rate, let loose upon the country at the end of each campaign. The inefficiency of the contemporary police system and the laxity, or worse, of the officials was startlingly illustrated by the robbery of the king's private treasure in 1303. When the king left Westminster in August 1302 he left a store of plate and jewels valued at £100,000 (equivalent to at least two millions of modern money) in charge of the monks of Westminster Abbey. The bulk of this was in the vaulted chamber now known as the Chapel of the Pyx but a certain number of hampers filled with plate were deposited in the cupboards of the Refectory. Hardly was the king's back turned when Richard de Podelicote, a pedlar, who had been watching his opportunity, broke into the Refectory and got away safely with a quantity of plate, the loss of which was either not noticed or hushed up. His appetite whetted by his success, Podelicote next undertook no less ambitious a scheme than the theft of the remainder of the treasure. With the connivance, if not the actual assistance, of the keeper of the Palace and of some of the monks he worked away steadily at night from Christmas 1302 till Easter 1303 and at last effected an entry and successfully carried off an enormous quantity of plate and jewels which were secreted in various places. The discovery of portions of the treasure lying about in the neighbourhood of the Abbey precincts, the appearance of royal plate in a number of goldsmiths' shops and the behaviour of the keeper and the monks aroused suspicion. A message was hurriedly sent to King Edward, then in Scotland; he promptly ordered enquiries to be made and as a result Podelicote and a number of those who had acted as receivers of the stolen property were hanged and others, including many of the monks, were imprisoned.

If this robbery was the most startling crime of the period it was by no means the most serious from the point of view of the community. In addition to what may be called the casual crime always existing where the grip of authority is loose there had grown up a regular organisation of crime. Throughout the country there were bands of ruffians, known from the clubs which they carried as "trailbastons", who made a trade of crime and were openly to be hired for assault or murder at a tariff which varied with the severity of the injury to be inflicted upon their victim. An order for an enquiry into these and other similar offences which had been committed and had remained unpunished since 24 June 1297 was the chief business of the parliament held at Westminster in March and April 1305. Edward also consulted with the Bishop of Glasgow and Robert Bruce, Earl of Carrick, now by the death of his father head of his family, as to the settlement of Scotland and by their advice arranged for a meeting of the Scottish representatives at Perth to elect two bishops, two abbots, two earls, two barons and two commoners who should meet him at Westminster and draw up a form of government for Scotland. At the end of April Edward left Westminster; June was spent in Surrey and Sussex, and while the court was at Midhurst on Sunday, 13 June Bishop Langton took occasion to reprove the Prince of Wales for his extravagance and ill behaviour; the Prince retorted with insults and abuse. Edward was not the man to put up with such misconduct even in the heir to the throne and promptly banished his son to Windsor, stopping his allowance and depriving him of the company of his favourite Piers de Gaveston.

The one source of danger in Scotland appeared to be William Wallace, who was still at large and, although a hunted outlaw with a price upon his head, was known to have such a hold upon the affections and imagination of the common people that there was good reason to fear his ability to stir up another rising. About the end of July this cause of anxiety was removed by his capture near Glasgow through the treachery of one of his followers whom he had offended. He was at once sent to London, where he arrived on 22 August. Next day he was taken to Westminster Hall, crowned with laurel in mockery of his entirely imaginary ambition of sovereignty, and was tried, or rather condemned, by a special commission appointed for the purpose. The charges of treason, robbery, murder and arson required no elaborate proofs; they were matters of common notoriety, and were admitted by the prisoner, save that he repudiated the name of traitor on the ground that he had never sworn allegiance to King Edward. The verdict was inevitable and the usual sentence for high treason, that he should be drawn, hanged and quartered was passed and at once executed upon him. Having been dragged at a horse's tail through the city to Tyburn he was hanged, cut down while still alive and disembowelled, his acts of sacrilege being avenged by the casting of his heart, from which these wicked thoughts and acts had emanated, into the flames. His head was struck off and set on London Bridge, while the quarters of his body were sent to Newcastle, Berwick, Stirling and Perth. The punishment of Wallace was terrible but it was not shocking or unjustified, it was no perversion of justice and that it was exceptional in severity is merely evidence that Edward did not often execute upon his fallen enemies the full measure of vengeance which contemporary law and public opinion would have regarded as justifiable. Five weeks after Wallace's execution, on 15 September 1305, the ten Scottish delegates came to Westminster and with the assistance of twenty English councillors appointed by Edward drew up a set of regulations for the government of Scotland. The ancient Scottish laws of the Highlands or Celtic districts were to give place to those passed or modified by King David and other kings, which were to be codified, such as were "plainly against God and reason" (i.e. English law) being rejected. Arrangements were made for the separate judicial administration of Lothian, the Lowlands, Galloway and the Highlands and for the preservation of the peace throughout the country. The king's nephew John of Brittany, to whom the king had given the earldom of Richmond, was appointed Warden of Scotland, with a council of Scots to assist him and sheriffs were appointed for the various counties. The regulations were as good as could well have been devised and were duly confirmed by King Edward, who received the homage of the Scottish delegates at Shene early in October and as an additional mark of favour extended the terms for the payment of ransoms due under the treaty of the previous year.

About this time, on 4 October, Edward sent a letter to the recently elected Pope politely declining the invitation to attend his coronation. With the letter he sent a handsome present of gold plate from his own royal table. The new Pope, Clement V, had been elected on 5 June, when the papal see had been vacant for nearly a year, Pope Boniface's successor, Benedict XI having died in July 1304 after a brief six months' tenure of the papacy. Pope Clement, who owed his election to King Philip IV and, as a Gascon and Archbishop of Bordeaux at the time of his election, was a subject of Edward I, was naturally very much more complaisant towards the two kings than Pope Boniface had been. Although Edward did not attend his coronation at Lyons, which was marred by the sudden fall of a wall overburdened with spectators, causing the death of the aged Duke of Brittany, he despatched an influential embassy to represent him and to discuss the question of a new crusade and other more practical and important matters. The immediate result of this embassy was the issue of a bull on 29 December 1305, which reached the king at Canford in

Dorset on 11 February 1306, absolving him from the oaths which he had sworn with regard to the Great Charter and the Forest Charter and prohibiting any future enforcement of them without the special sanction of the papal authority. On the strength of this Edward on 27 May 1306 issued a new Forest Statute in which he calmly revoked all the disafforestments which he had sworn to observe and made a great show of magnanimity by remitting all penalties for forest offences committed in the disafforested lands.

This breach of faith might have raised a storm, but the natural leader of the opposition to the king's dishonesty was absent. Archbishop Winchelsey, the champion of the papacy, had been suspended from office and summoned to appear before the papal court in March; betrayed by the ally he had served so faithfully he turned to his old opponent, but Edward was in no generous mood and answered him with abuse and reproaches. Moreover, the king wrote to Pope Clement making fresh complaints against Winchelsey and, with his usual opportune enthusiasm for the Holy Land, accusing him of being the chief obstacle in the way of a new crusade. The Pope showed his good will towards Edward by detaining the archbishop at Bordeaux and his zeal for the Holy Land by bestowing upon the courtly and wealthy Bishop Anthony Bek of Durham the magnificent and empty title of Patriarch of Jerusalem. Not only was the chief opponent of the king absent but the nation had other matters than forests to occupy its mind at the moment. Scotland, which had seemed so peacefully settled, was once more in revolt. When in 1302 the Scots had risen under the leadership of John Comyn of Badenoch, Robert Bruce, not wishing to assist a movement which, if successful, would place Balliol or his nephew Comyn on the throne of Scotland, took arms on the English side. He was rewarded after the pacification of the country by being appointed one of the wardens of

Scotland and promptly began to intrigue with the Bishop of Glasgow and other prominent patriots who had accepted positions of trust under the English king. Having gained considerable support he made an appointment with Comyn in the church of the Friars Minors at Dumfries on 10 February 1306 and there endeavoured to persuade him to join the revolt under his leadership. The Red Comyn was no friend of Bruce, they had come to blows on a previous occasion, and he refused to fall in with his plans. Enraged and fearful that he would betray the plot, Bruce drew his dagger and stabbed the Comyn, his followers completing the murder. Almost at once the whole country rose for Bruce and on 25 March he was crowned king at Scone by the Bishops of Glasgow and St. Andrews, the further ceremony of installation being performed by the Countess of Buchan, without her husband's knowledge, as daughter of the Earl of Fife, to whom the privilege of performing that rite belonged.

King Edward was making a prolonged stay at Winchester when news of the murder of the Red Comyn reached him. His health was failing and it was possibly due to a presentiment that he might not live to execute the vengeance that he threatened against Bruce that he determined to bestow the dignity of knighthood upon his son and heir. Orders were issued immediately after Easter (3 April, 1306) for preparations for that ceremony to be made, and all persons of suitable position who wished to be knighted at the same time were told to make proper application, the date fixed being Whit Sunday, 22 May. Before that day, on 4 May, Queen Margaret gave birth to another child, which proved to be a daughter, though the king appears to have made up his mind that it would be a son, as on the previous 28 December he had sent an offering to the shrine of St. Richard at Chichester "on behalf of his son Sir Richard, as yet unborn". Finding that it was a girl he had her

christened Eleanor and, with his inveterate tendency to
match-making, within four days of her birth opened
negotiations for her marriage to Robert, son of the Duke
of Burgundy. On 20 May the old king reached Westminster, where had assembled more than two hundred
and fifty young nobles desirous of the honour of knighthood. On Whit Sunday Edward bestowed the coveted
honour upon the Prince of Wales and invested him with
the Duchy of Aquitaine; the Prince then went into the
Abbey and at the high altar dubbed the other candidates,
most of whom had kept their ceremonial vigil the previous night in the Temple Church. The ceremony was
brought to a close in the usual manner with a great
banquet at which the king, who had wisely avoided the
densely thronged Abbey, presided. During the entertainment two great swans covered with a network of gold
and little bells, most wonderful to behold, were brought
in. As the eyes of all the guests were fixed upon these
swans King Edward uttered a vow, "By the God of
Heaven and these swans", to avenge the death of Comyn
and the perfidy of the Scots in life or death, calling upon
his son and the nobles to swear that if he died before the
task was accomplished they would carry his body with the
army and not bury it until full vengeance had been wrought
upon the Scots. To this demand the assembled company
answered with a shout of assent and acclamation.

Three days after the great festivity of Whitsun, while
most of the thousand knights who, with their retinues had
filled every corner of London and Westminster, were still
present, two of the king's granddaughters were married,
Joan of Bar to the young John de Warenne, Earl of
Surrey, and Eleanor de Clare to Hugh le Despenser. On
5 June a papal bull denouncing the murder of Comyn
was publicly read at St. Paul's Cross, as well as that which
revoked the king's oath to observe the Forest Charter,
and the parliament broke up, the magnates hurrying off
to prepare for the Scottish expedition. The young

Prince of Wales paid a hurried visit to Winchester to take leave of Queen Margaret, who appears to have won the affection of all her step-children, and then hastened back to precede his father towards the north. Age was telling upon the king and his health was failing; he was obliged to travel in a litter by short stages and his anxiety was shown by the quantity of offerings sent on his behalf to the chief shrines in England and even abroad to St. Denis at Pontigny, to St. Leonard at Limoges, St. Eutropius at Saintes and the Three Kings at Cologne. Unbroken in spirit, however, he insisted upon accompanying the army and had reached Hexham Priory on 15 August when he received the welcome news of the capture of Sir Simon Fraser, next to Bruce the most famous and dangerous of the rebels.* This marked the culmination of the first act of the campaign. Forces under Aymer de Valence, Henry Percy and Robert Clifford had been sent forward in the middle of May and had gained a considerable success over Bruce at Methven, close to Perth, on 19 June. The Bishops of Glasgow and St. Andrews and the Abbot of Scone had already been captured and sent back in fetters to English prisons. Another defeat in August broke up Bruce's little army and he himself fled to the island of Rathlin. His wife and daughter fell into Edward's hands shortly afterwards; the former as daughter of the loyal Earl of Ulster and an unwilling participant in her husband's schemes was sent to the royal manor of Brustwick and treated with honourable courtesy but Bruce's daughter Marjory and his sisters Christine Seton and Elizabeth Siward were placed in close custody in English nunneries. The Countess of Buchan, who had installed Bruce as king, was placed in a lattice cage in one of the towers of Berwick Castle and King Robert's sister Mary was similarly confined at Roxburgh. Of the leaders who were

*A long ballad on the capture and execution of Fraser is given in Wright's *Political Songs* (Camden Soc.) 213–234.

captured Fraser and the Earl of Atholl suffered as traitors
in London, Neil Bruce at Berwick and Christopher Seton
and his two brothers at Dumfries. While Edward was thus
acting with severity towards the leaders of the rebellion
his son at the head of the young knights, who had been
sent to earn their spurs in the Lowlands, was acting with
ruthless cruelty towards the poor inhabitants, for which
he was sternly rebuked by his father. A more serious
quarrel between the two Edwards took place in the
spring of 1307 when the Prince dared to ask leave to
bestow his county of Ponthieu upon his beloved Piers
de Gaveston. Furiously the old king turned on him,
seizing him by the hair and exclaiming, "Whoreson, mis-
begotten boy, wilt thou give away lands who has never
gained any? As God liveth, if it were not for fear of
breaking up the kingdom, thou shouldst never enjoy
thy heritage." To prevent any such suggestion being made
again he made Gaveston swear never to accept any lands
from the Prince and to abjure the realm, also taking a
corroborative oath from his son.

Edward's health had improved with the better news
from Scotland and at Newbrough on 30 August he caused
a special mass to be celebrated in thanksgiving for his
recovery; but he was not in a fit condition to take an
active part in the expedition and from the beginning of
October to the end of February 1307 he lay at Lanercost
Priory, where the queen had joined him. In March he
moved to Carlisle, where a parliament had been summoned. The action of the pope in claiming for three years
the first fruits of all vacant benefices and in sending over
an agent, William de Testa, to take charge of the province
of Canterbury during Winchelsey's suspension had
roused so much resentment that although Edward had
been willing to permit these papal encroachments for the
sake of keeping Winchelsey out of the way, he could not
resist the strong protests of parliament. Testa was forbidden to act and the ordinance passed in 1305 but never

published, forbidding the export of money from English monasteries to foreign chapters, was now issued. The king, under the influence of Cardinal Pedro of Spain, who had come to arrange for the marriage of the Prince of Wales, revoked the action taken against Testa "so far as in him lay" but the Council interpreted this reservation as not overruling the parliamentary prohibitions and prevented Testa from acting.

Meanwhile, in February 1307, Bruce had returned to the attack. A landing by his brothers Thomas and Alexander in the west had resulted in their defeat, capture and execution, but King Robert, after attempting to retake his own castle of Carrick from Sir Henry de Percy, had won a slight success over Aymer de Valence at Loudun Hill and a more decided victory over Edward's son-in-law, Monthermer of Gloucester, at Ayr. Determined to take the field himself Edward once more mounted his horse on 3 July. He was hardly able to ride more than two or three miles in the day and had only reached Burgh-on-the-Sands on 6 July. The next day, as he was being raised up to take some food he fell back dead.

The dead king's body was brought slowly southwards, reaching Waltham Abbey on 4 August. Here it remained, while constant services were celebrated by detachments of monks from all the great monasteries, till 27 October, when it was buried in Westminster Abbey, the last mass being celebrated by Anthony Bek, Bishop of Durham.

"And it is to be hoped and most confidently believed that the innumerable good works which he wrought during his life shall bear witness on his behalf before the tribunal of Jesus Christ, that he may reign with him for ever. Amen."

# Chapter Nine

# Character of Edward

It was said that the last instruction of the dying king to his son were that his body should be embalmed and carried with the army and not buried until Scotland had been reduced to subjection; but it is not improbable that these orders, if they were ever given, were subsequently modified by the king himself and that his burial in Westminster Abbey under a plain marble slab was due neither to the disobedience nor the meanness of Edward II. A later generation engraved upon the tomb the words *Pactum Serva* and modern historians have commented with varying degrees of irony upon the appropriateness of the motto 'Keep Faith' to the king who threw over the treaty of Brigham, obtained crusading subsidies on false pretences and endeavoured to evade fulfilling his oath to confirm the charters. It is, however, permissible to suggest that the plain marble and the motto, which may well have been re-engraved at a later date, were intended by Edward to be a stern and simple reminder to his son and his nobles of the oath which they had sworn with him upon the swans to reduce Scotland to subjection. On no other hypothesis is it easy to explain the strange simplicity and insignificance of the monument which marks the resting-place of one who was distinguished among his contemporaries for the magnificence with which he adorned the tombs of his own friends. To the enrichment of his father's tomb he bestowed jewels which he had brought from France, the monument of his brother Edmund is one of the gems of Westminster

Queen Eleanor

Winchelsea

Abbey, while that to Eleanor of Castile with the accompanying series of crosses constitutes a memorial unrivalled in beauty or splendour. Constantly in the course of his progresses we find him giving hangings of cloth of gold to adorn the tombs of his relations or friends, such as Patrick de Chaworth, the Countess of Hereford or the Vicomte of Tarcazin. Faithfulness to those whom he had once admitted into the rather narrow circle of his friendship was, indeed, a mark of his character. Those whom he had once found loyal and capable as ministers, soldiers or diplomats retained, as a rule, his confidence to the end; markedly was this the case with his ministers: Robert Burnel, the trusted adviser of his youth, remained his adviser after his accession and held the chancellorship for eighteen years without a break and to Walter de Langton, his successor, he extended a similarly unwavering support. While Henry II on the death of an official who had served him faithfully, even to the sacrifice of his conscience, could contemptuously commend his soul to the Devil, Edward was lavish in the bestowal of alms and the celebration of masses for the souls of his servants.

Remarkable as was the resemblance in some ways between Edward I and his great-grandfather Henry II the difference in their attitude towards religion was as great as the difference in appearance between the tall, dark, wiry Plantagenet and the short, stout, ruddy Angevin. Henry was as nearly an agnostic as even a king dared be in the twelfth century, while Edward was a man of very sincere piety. Not only did his affectionate regard for the dead take the form of having masses celebrated for the good of their souls, but it was also his constant custom to testify his gratitude to God and the saints by the celebration of masses, at one time "for the good news which he had received from France", at another "for news of the taking of a certain knight", or for the good news of the landing of his affianced bride, Margaret of

M

France, or again "out of special devotion for his recovery from illness". And as religious services marked the successful termination of his difficulties so also when faced by any crisis he sought the aid of the saints and of the prayers of the faithful. During his Welsh expeditions, while negotiating with the French, before starting on his Scottish campaigns, and on other occasions he desired the prayers of the Franciscan Order, or of certain monasteries, or of the whole Church, even soliciting the prayers of the Church at the very time that he was most actively attacking the representatives of that Church—the clergy—on the subject of subsidies. In all his Scottish campaigns the sacred banners of St. John of Beverley and St. Cuthbert of Durham accompanied his hosts and the standards of St. George, St. Edward and St. Edmund floated side by side with the leopards of England. With him on all his journeyings, after it had fallen into his hands with the taking of Carnarvon in 1283, went the Cross Neith, or Rood of St. Neot, a portion of the True Cross which had been the most sacred and revered relic of the Welsh; and to this was added, some ten years later, the Black Rood of Scotland, a relic, similar in nature and veneration, taken from Edinburgh. Moreover, before each expedition it was his almost invariable practice to visit certain shrines, particularly St. Edmund's and Walsingham, to whose miraculous Virgin he expressed an especial devotion. To his name saint, the Confessor, he naturally showed due respect and St. Albans, Ely and the shrines of St. Richard at Chichester and St. Thomas Cantelupe at Hereford were also distinguished by frequent marks of his devotion. The most famous and popular of all English saints, St. Thomas of Canterbury, could not be ignored but Edward does not seem to have shown any great affection for him and one cannot help feeling that he was too conscious of the parallel between Becket and his own troublesome archbishops to display any great devotion towards the martyr.

Towards the Church on earth Edward's attitude was respectful but far from uncritical. While he recognized the moral superiority of the clergy and that, as he expressed it when licensing one of his bondmen to receive holy orders, "it befits the king to favour those who, inspired by divine grace, forsake the cares and pleasures of this world to serve the King of Kings", he would not tolerate the clerical claim to make the best of both worlds by evading their responsibilities to the state and laying up treasure in this life as well as in the next. For the monastic orders he had no great admiration and it was with great reluctance that he allowed his daughter Mary to take the veil at Amesbury; when in the course of a progress or pilgrimage he visited any monastery it is true that he made offerings at the principal altars and shrines on a fairly lavish scale but his gifts practically never took the form of endowments of land and his legislation, in the Statute *De Religiosis*, aimed expressly at restricting the expansion of the monastic estates. One monastery, founded first at Dernhale and afterwards transferred to Vale Royal, owed its foundation to a vow which he had uttered while in peril of shipwreck in the days before he ascended the throne. Another, that of Meynan in Wales, was built at his expense, but only because the Cistercian convent established there had been removed from Conway to make room for his new castle. Towards the rebuilding of the other Welsh abbey of Strata Florida after it had been burnt by his troops he also subscribed liberally, just as in similar circumstances he had promised a thousand marks for the rebuilding on a more magnificent scale and a better site of the Cathedral and close of St. Asaph. But Edward cannot be considered as by any means a patron of monasticism, though a curious entry of payments in 1299 "for the King's robe of Sempringham" seems to imply that he had been received into the fraternity of that purely English order as a kind of honorary canon.

For the friars, on the other hand, he had far more sympathy. Whenever he passed through or near a town where any of the four orders of Friars was established it was his rule to send them money sufficient for their food for one or more days, on the basis of 3d. a day for each friar. Towards the expenses of their provincial or general chapters he was also a generous subscriber and while in Paris in 1286 he attended the chapter general of the Dominicans on several occasions. In this attitude he was supported both by Eleanor of Castile and by Archbishop Pecham, himself a friar and therefore no lenient critic of the monks. The feeling between the monks and friars is brought out in the protest of Pecham against the establishment of the Cistercians from Conway within the bishopric of St. Asaph where there were already four abbeys of White Monks; "For though they may be good men, if God please, still they are the hardest neighbours that prelates and parsons could have. For where they plant their foot they destroy towns, take away tithes and curtail by their privileges all the power of prelacy." On their side the monks, deprived by the popularity of the friars of rich mortuaries and fees for burials, obits and anniversaries, retorted by calling the friars body-snatchers and comparing them to dogs yelping for bits of dead bodies. In the undignified and greedy hunt after dead men's leavings even the secular canons were not above sharing, if we may judge from the complaint of Henry and James de Grandison that they had been cheated out of the lands which should have descended to them from their brother, the Bishop of Verdun, by the canons of his cathedral, who came to his funeral "not to pray for his soul but to prey on his goods" (*non ad orandum sed ad devorandum*).

Of the king's attitude towards the Pope a good deal has been said in the preceding chapters. While any such idea as that of an independent Church of England was inconceivable at this period, the English branch of the

Catholic Church was distinctly less submissive to the central control of Rome than most of the continental branches. Edward, while tacitly admitting the religious supremacy of the Pope, had no intention of allowing papal interference in temporal matters; his dealings with Pedro of Aragon were not influenced by papal denunciations of that king as excommunicate and deposed; when Pope Boniface VIII inserted in the bull appointing William de Geynesburgh to the bishopric of Worcester a clause investing him with the temporalities of the see, Edward made the bishop renounce the clause and fined him 1,000 marks for accepting the bull, and to the culminating impudence of the papal claim to dispose of the Scottish throne Edward and his barons gave an unqualified refusal. If on the one hand the king had, for financial and other reasons, to exercise caution in his attempts to curb papal pretensions, on the other hand the popes had to submit to much that they would have resented if it had not been for fear of offending the only possible leader of the new crusade, with the idea of which they were obsessed. Doubts of Edward's good faith in his constantly renewed, and as constantly postponed, vows of going on crusade must have arisen, but, in view of the undoubted fact that without his active assistance any attempt at renewing the crusades was bound to fail, the popes could only hope that he would eventually fulfil his promises. For the leadership of such an expedition he was marked out alike by his experience and by his reputation as a warrior.

As a warrior his reputation was well established and well deserved, not the least important of his qualifications being that mysterious attribute known as luck, an attribute inspiring alike to the possessor and to those serving under him. At the time of his death a panegyrist applied to King Edward the words of St. Paul "in perils often" and commented upon the dangers which he had encountered by sea and land and his constant narrow escapes from death. More than once he was in danger of shipwreck; as a young man he was playing chess on one occasion with a knight when he was suddenly moved, by the Blessed Virgin of Walsingham, as he believed, to get up and walk away, thus escaping a great stone which crashed down from the vault a moment later upon the seat he had been occupying; in Palestine he survived the murderous attack of the assassin by almost a miracle; in Paris the lightning passed over his shoulder and slew two of his attendants; at Winchelsea when his horse leapt the town wall he was uninjured; at the siege of Stirling a bolt from a crossbow struck his saddle as he rode un-armed and a stone from a mangonel brought his horse to the ground. Even illness seemed to pass him by and his last years found him as vigorous and upright as a palm tree with eyes and brain undimmed and the teeth still firm in his jaws, able to bite hard literally as well as figuratively, at the table as in the field. Add to this element of the luck which turns the scale the right way at the critical moment a cool foresight, personal courage and a life's training on the battle-fields of Britain, the continent and the Holy Land, and it is not surprising that Edward should have proved a great and successful general.

In the matter of actual field tactics there is no particular evidence that Edward excelled; of the three tactically most important battles of the reign, in which skilful use was made of the bowmen in conjunction with the cavalry, Orewin Bridge may be attributed to John Giffard, who may well have been responsible for the use of similar tactics in the battle near Conway in 1294 although the actual commander was the Earl of Warwick. At the third battle, Falkirk, Edward was in command, but the use of the bowmen, which decided the battle, seems to have been something of an afterthought. But while we cannot credit the king with any exceptional brilliance or originality in tactics we may accord him admiration for his skill in organisation. The care with which arrangements were made for the Welsh expeditions; the deliberate preparation for his advance by the clearing of roads through the forests; the co-operation of the fleet for purposes of transport; all these are marks of that genius which is a talent for taking pains. Moreover in Edward's hands the constitution of the army was altered in several important ways. At the beginning of his reign the king was dependent for his heavy cavalry, the most valued and important arm, upon the service due from his military tenants. Theoretically the crown was entitled to the service, for forty days, of between six and seven thousand knights; to call up this complete force at any one time could never have been feasible and the evidence of records goes to show that Edward I could not rely upon obtaining more than about a fifteenth of this total, say 400 knights or their equivalent, two of the lighter armed serjeants-at-arms or troopers being accepted for one knight. From the defaulting fees fines were exacted, or demanded, on varying scales and the feudal obligation was further extended by orders compelling all persons possessing lands worth £20 yearly to take up the privileged responsibility of knighthood. Young men also to whom the adventurous life of the soldier appealed were encouraged to apply for knighthood and were equipped by the king. The force of cavalry thus brought together by feudal summons was inevitably a heterogeneous body composed of units of very varying size, lacking cohesion and discipline and liable to dwindle rapidly away as the forty days of each unit came to an end. To remedy this last defect it was the custom for the king to keep on at his own cost such troops as were willing to serve for wages beyond the period of their feudal service. Edward extended this system and largely replaced the feudal levies by mercenaries, raising the bulk of his cavalry as paid soldiers. By this means he was able to brigade them under approved and responsible officers and to introduce discipline. The infantry were raised on the militia system, a demand for a certain number of men being sent to the sheriffs of certain counties, who, probably through the organisation of the hundreds and tithings, selected the required number of men from the ranks of the yeomen and peasantry. They were armed partly at their own expense and partly at the cost of the county and received wages, at the rate of unskilled labourers, from the day of their mobilisation, except when they were called out in defence of their own county, in which case they were not paid. They were organised in companies of a hundred under centenars, each of whom had under him five vintenars, or section-commanders; by a later development the companies were grouped in battalions of a thousand men under a millenar. Their equipment for the most part consisted of knives, swords and pikes and occasionally some badge or uniform was worn, brassards with the cross of St. George being used in at least one instance, while in 1295 the troops enrolled in East Anglia were given white tunics from which they received the nickname of "Blaunchecotes".

An important branch of the infantry was the bowmen and it was by his development of this arm that Edward obtained many of his successes and paved the way for the future glories of Crécy and Agincourt. Although the longbow was in use for sporting purposes and found a place in the Assize of Arms of Henry III it was not looked upon with favour by military authorities; it had not attained to anything like the size, strength and accuracy of the longbows used a generation later and was considered much inferior to the crossbow, which itself was unpopular with the more conservative and scrupulous soldiers as an unchivalrous and murderous weapon, on which grounds its use had been forbidden by the Lateran Council of 1139. The natural result of such a condemnation had been to advertise the formidable properties of the crossbow; its use had been brought to a high pitch of excellence by the godless mercenaries of Gascony and it was upon these expert ruffians that Edward largely depended for his bowmen. Three types of these bows, which were made of yew, horn or whalebone, were in use; the small common crossbow "of one foot", in which the purchase for stringing the bow was obtained by the archer placing his foot in a ring at the end of the bow; the larger bow "of two feet" the stringing of which required the whole weight of the archer; and the later and largest type, the bow *ad turnum*, in which the string was brought over the trigger by the action of a winch. Immense numbers of quarrels or bolts for these crossbows were issued from the arsenals of the Tower, St. Briavels and Bristol and they formed the principal weapon of the castle garrisons. Of the archers, or longbowmen, far the greater number were mercenaries from South Wales, but there were also picked bodies of English archers from Sherwood Forest and the Peak. In addition to the purely combatant infantry there were bodies of woodmen, miners, masons and carpenters employed in erecting defences, temporary or permanent, road and bridge-making, and the construction of the artillery of the period, the great siege engines which under Edward I attained dimensions unknown to his predecessors. These engineers, as we may call them, were recruited by compulsion but were paid the wages of skilled labourers.

In these days, when we have become inured to reading of 50,000 casualties in a single battle, it is strange to realise that 10,000 infantry and 2,000 cavalry constituted the average English army at its full strength towards the end of Edward's reign. Earlier in his reign the numbers were usually smaller. On one occasion, in 1298, all records were eclipsed by the assembly of a force of over 20,000 on the Scottish border, but such a force was unwieldy and the quality of its component troops varied inversely with the quantity, so this particular army was speedily disbanded, having effected practically nothing. Even with the normal army of half that size the full strength was only maintained for a short period. Apart from other causes military service was usually unpopular and desertions from the infantry were numerous and occasionally wholesale. In particular the recruits obtained by the practice in vogue during the last twelve years of the reign of issuing pardons to criminals and jail-birds if they would join the army proved unreliable and deserted in great numbers. Even where the county officers picked their men carefully, which was by no means always the case, there must have been a considerable proportion of raw ill-equipped men. Taking everything into consideration, and allowing for the troops employed in guarding communications or on independent operations, we may say that a fighting force of anything over 5,000 constituted a formidable army. The garrisons of the castles also were on a scale which seems surprisingly small; from thirty to sixty men for such great fortresses as Edward's splendid Welsh castles of Harlech, Conway and Carnarvon seems an absurdly inefficient figure, and even the 180 crossbowmen and archers of Newcastle, an exceptionally large force, do not seem sufficient for so vital a stronghold during the critical situation of 1297. Allowance, however, has probably to be made for the unpaid assistance of local levies and refugees and still more for the mere passive strength of the walls, the city of Carlisle on one occasion, as has been mentioned, being successfully defended against the assaults of the Scots by the women almost unaided. In all military matters, therefore, of this period it is essential to adjust our focus, to remember the relatively minute scale of operations and, above all to base all estimates on records, such as muster rolls and paymasters' accounts, rather than on the wild assertions of imaginative historians.

Apart from his military ability as organiser and commander Edward had courage and skill in actual combat and delighted in the rough sport of the tournament. We have seen that as a young man he paid several visits to France in search of such adventures and that on his way back from Palestine he took part in "the little Battle of Châlons", gaining no little glory therefrom. That he continued after his coronation to take actual part in tournaments is not quite clear, but he certainly encouraged them and was present at many. In the autumn of 1279 a great joust or "Round Table" of a hundred knights was held by Roger Mortimer at Kenilworth and King Edward wrote to Philip of France asking him to excuse Sir John de Prye, a French knight, for having taken part in it, on the ground that as it was taking place while he was passing through England he had only acted as befitted a knight. On another occasion Edward again wrote to Philip, who had issued an ordinance against tournaments, asking him to allow Sir John de Nesle to come over and take part in tournaments which were being got up for the entertainment of the Duke of Brabant. To celebrate the successful conclusion of the Welsh campaign in 1284 a great "Round Table" was held at Nevyn in North Wales, in spite of the protests of Archbishop Pecham against the waste of blood and money which might better have been devoted to a crusade, and two years later we find Edward providing an outfit for his nephew John of Brittany to attend tournaments at Bedford and Croydon. Amongst other similar entertainments we may mention that held at Winchester to celebrate the king's marriage to Margaret of France and the "Round Table" held by Edward's orders in January 1302 at Falkirk after the conclusion of the truce with Scotland. Like his great-grandfather, Edward was never so happy as when on horseback and a large part was played in his life by the twin sports of hunting and hawking. To his courtiers his energy in the laying out of parks and preserves seemed admirable, though his desperate endeavours to evade the restrictions of the Forest Charter and extend the sporting rights of the crown at their expense were naturally regarded with disfavour. Those who wished to win his favour gave him presents of horses, sporting hounds or hawks, and such were the presents which he himself deemed fit for kings, whether they ruled in Aragon or in Armenia. Of his hawks it might be said they were treated "like Christians", and the colloquialism may be justified by the number of cases in which pilgrimages were undertaken for the health of sick falcons. Occasionally the birds themselves seem to have been carried to the shrines, of which that of St. Thomas Cantelupe of Hereford was the favourite, but more often waxen images of the hawks were sent to the shrine. Nor were these images rough and ready birdlike lumps of wax, for we find that their manufacture was entrusted to Adam, the king's chief goldsmith. Another and simpler method of invoking the aid of the saints was to bend a silver penny above the bird in honour of some saint, to whose altar the penny was then taken. Not only were pennies bent over the falcons but in 1278 we read of 32 pence bent over the same number of horses "in honour of St. Hippolitus"—the patron saint of horses. It is not without interest to notice that the same ceremony was observed in the case of the king himself in his last illness, two pence being bent over his head and sent to the shrine of St. Thomas Cantelupe.

In the matter of less strenuous forms of amusement we have evidence that Edward indulged in occasional games of skill. Reference has already been made to his miraculous escape from death when playing chess and there are other entries which show that he enjoyed that royal and ancient game. So also, no doubt, did Queen Eleanor, for in 1287 when the Visitor of the Order of the Temple presented Edward with a set of chessmen in crystal and jasper the king immediately gave them to his queen. Both Edward and Eleanor are also found playing "the game of Four Kings", which seems to have been a variety of chess, and dicing, though on a scale quite insignificant compared with the reckless gambling of their son Edward. There are also mentions of "tables", or backgammon, and "griasch", which may be the same as "creag", said to have been a kind of ninepins. More frivolous amusements were not despised by the warrior king. At Easter 1261, possibly to celebrate the completion of his twenty-fifth year, Edward and his knights had donned "queintis" or fancy dress, and in 1290 similar "queyntis" were provided for some of his knights and ladies in which to dance at the wedding of the Princess Margaret. A quaint custom also existed at the court by which if the queen's ladies caught the king in bed on Easter Monday he had to pay them a ransom—which he did on a lavish scale. In 1278 the "five damsels of the queen who caught the king on the morrow of Easter at Glastonbury" were given £6. 13s. 4d. "to buy ornaments for their heads"; nine years later £12 was given to "the damsels of the queen at Mauléon by the king's gift because they caught him in his bed on the morrow of Easter", and in 1290 as much as £14 was given "to seven ladies and damsels of the queen because they caught the king in his bed on the morrow of Easter and made him pay fine to them for the king's peace." Edward was a generous patron of the jesters, fools and buffoons who visited his court in the retinues of his royal and noble visitors and also to the humbler entertainers and strolling musicians. While in Gascony we find him providing a horse for the King of Aragon's female jester and giving money to "a little singing girl at Breteuil who did acrobatic feats", to "a young man who piped on the bagpipes" and to "a tumbling girl" at Bordeaux. On other occasions Maud Makejoye is rewarded for dancing before him, and money is given to two Germans for dancing jigs and to Bastin Noblet of Liége, acrobat, who came with Janyn le Get of Douai, minstrel. Payments to minstrels, in particular, are so numerous and generous that we may assume his fondness for music, and it is noteworthy that when the Prince of Wales was expecting a visit from the king and Queen Margaret at Langley in 1303 he had his organ repaired by Master John, organist to the Earl Warenne. That he was also a patron of literature seems less probable; no such claim was advanced on his behalf by any panegyrist and practically no trace of any purchases of books, other than missals and breviaries for use in his chapels, occurs in the accounts of his expenditure. That he understood, and occasionally spoke, English is almost certain but it may be doubted if his knowledge of Latin was extensive and it is significant that in the last year of his life he sent to his Chancellor a draft of a letter in French to the Pope with orders that it should be translated into Latin.

As a patron of art Edward could not be compared with his father. Henry III was in the habit of giving the most elaborate and minute orders for the adornment and decoration of his royal palaces; Edward seems to have been content to give general orders, though he had sufficient appreciation of what was good to entrust them to the best craftsmen of the period, a period at which the skill of the English artist-craftsmen had risen almost to its highest pitch of excellence. His justification is seen in such scanty fragments as have survived of the works executed for him, notably the beautiful monument of Queen Eleanor. Architecturally his energies were devoted almost entirely to military works, and the stately ruins of Carnarvon, Conway, Harlech and Beaumaris bear striking evidence to the skill of his military architects and their instinctive ability to combine strength of construction with beauty of line. Of examples of metalwork we have little that can be connected in any way with Edward, with the single exception of a number of seals, of which those used by Queen Margaret can be ascribed definitely to William de Keyles, goldsmith and sealmaker of London, who received 10 marks for making the queen's great seal of silver and her privy seal of gold. In the many inventories that have survived we may read tantalisingly long lists of jewels, gold and enamelled cups and other treasures which have long vanished. We would give much to see the "noble shield of steel adorned with various devices" (*diversimodo depicto*) which King Charles of Sicily sent to King Edward by the hands of Huguet le Armurer, the silver model of a ship which Edward gave to Queen Margaret, or the girdle of red silk adorned with 25 cameos, which figures in the regalia with the great crown, valued at £400, four other crowns, including "a beautiful one with rubies and emeralds", coronets, garlands, a chaplet of rubies and other jewels. While Edward maintained a becoming magnificence of state he was in his personal tastes simple and averse to display, dressing plainly and rightly relying upon his character and personality rather than upon kingly trappings to uphold his dignity. His dislike of ceremony, coupled with his passion for sport, gave him a distaste for town life and he rarely honoured the larger towns with his presence for more than a few days unless compelled by exigences of business.

For London in particular he appears to have had a rooted dislike, dating from the days when at Lewes he avenged upon the Londoners their insults to his mother, and his residence at Westminster, therefore, practically always implies a parliament or other business of state. To Edward, as autocrat, independent citizens ranked with recalcitrant barons and presumptuous prelates as dangerous rivals to be kept in their proper place and he was not averse to reading them a lesson when opportunity arose. In 1285 the Justices sitting at the Tower attempted to override the privileges of the city and summoned the Mayor, Gregory de Rokesle, before them. Rokesle called a meeting of the aldermen and, in order to avoid on the one hand disobedience to the summons and on the other prejudice to the office of mayor, resigned his office, handing the seal to Stephen Ashwy, and appeared as a simple alderman before the Justices, to whom he maintained that the citizens were not obliged to enter the Tower for the purpose of sitting on inquests or to attend the court without forty days' notice. To this John de Kirkby made the illogical but conclusive retort of seizing the liberties of the city into the king's hands on the ground that the constitution of the city had been set aside through there being no mayor. For thirteen years London remained without a mayor, under the control of Sir Ralph de Sandwich, and it was not until, on his return from the unfortunate Flemish expedition in 1298, Edward felt the necessity of conciliating the wealthy and powerful citizens that he restored the forfeited liberties.

Towards the other great cities, little inferior to the capital in wealth and influence, Edward's attitude was similarly repressive. The liberties of York were seized for some unstated offence and only restored on payment of a fine of 1,000 marks in 1283; those of Norwich were forfeited about the same time on the ground that certain criminals tried by the local court had been arrested outside the borough boundary, and in 1285 the community of Bristol were fined £500 for some legal offence. At the same time Edward's prejudice against towns was not blind; he encouraged, as we have seen, their growth in Wales and he was directly responsible for the laying out of two seaports. The "ancient town" of Winchelsea, a member of the great confederacy of the Cinque Ports, was suffering from the inroads of the sea at least as early as 1281 when Edward took measures to secure land in the neighbouring manor of Iham to be leased for building purposes to the "barons" (as the freemen of the Ports were called). Two years later Stephen de Penchester, warden of the Cinque Ports, Henry le Waleys and Gregory de Rokesle were commissioned to lay out the new town of Iham to replace Winchelsea, already in great part submerged; they were to plan the streets and select places for the market and for two churches, to be dedicated, like those of the old town, in honour of St. Thomas and St. Giles. The result of their operations was the creation of a town, unique in medieval England in being planned strictly on the ancient Roman system of blocks of houses separated by parallel series of roads crossing at right angles, a system also employed in the *bastides*, or fortified towns of southern France. A great storm in 1287, which wrought fearful havoc on the south and eastern coast, completed the destruction of old Winchelsea and it was below the walls of this new Winchelsea that the great fleet assembled in 1297. The second town for which Edward was responsible was that founded in the mouth of the Humber on the little river called the Hull and from its royal origin was known as Kingston-upon-Hull. In this case the town, which was established during the opening years of the fourteenth century, was not laid out on any definite plan; there was no population waiting to inhabit it and it was allowed to grow up gradually, being still in its infancy when its royal founder died.

The renewal and confirmation of their charters granted to many towns under Edward I, as in all other reigns, so far from being a mark of his favour may with equal justice be read as reminders to the citizens that they held their privileges by grace of the crown—a grace for the continuation of which they had to pay. For trading communities Edward had little sympathy; the merchants were useful to him as the English sheep were to the merchants, because they could be fleeced upon occasion, but "the flower of chivalry" can have felt as little admiration for trade as any Japanese *samurai*. While trade and industry were thus left, as a whole, to develop, unhelped and unhindered by royal action, Edward occasionally interfered in municipal matters on behalf of the poorer members of the community. Jealous of his own prerogative, Edward had no intention of allowing any class of his subjects to imitate his example by extending their privileges at the expense of their subordinates and in several instances he interfered to prevent the exploitation

N

of the poorer citizens by their wealthy brethren. On no fewer than three occasions he ordered enquiry to be made into the action of the governing body at Lincoln; in 1276 it was alleged that the whole of a fine of 500 marks inflicted on the community had been levied from eleven citizens—who cannot, it is true, have been poor but were apparently unpopular; in 1286 when a rate was to be raised for paving the city, the king expressly ordered that the poor should not be made to contribute; and in 1290 complaint was made that a fine assessed on the rich, for concealing goods of the banished Jews, had been extorted from the poor. At Cambridge in 1291, at Lynn in 1305 and elsewhere on other occasions the rich were accused of shifting their burdens on to the shoulders of the poor. It was Edward's policy to repress the rich and gain the support of the poorer classes, who might act as a drag upon the ambitions of their wealthier neighbours but were in little danger of obtaining too much power themselves; but in addition to policy he was urged on this course by a distinct appreciation of justice for its own sake and by a sense of sympathy for the poor, which we may be sure was encouraged by the gracious Eleanor. Following his father's example, Edward was generous in the bestowal of alms: every Sunday 666 poor persons were fed, at a cost of $1\frac{1}{2}$d. a head, and on feast days similar free meals were provided for varying numbers, ranging from 100 to 1,300, the seventeenth birthday of Prince Edward being celebrated by the feeding of 1,700 poor. A more personal and individual touch occurs in the entry of gifts "to a poor man at Pershore", "to a poor English scholar chaunting at Solak", "to a poor clerk attached to the court, going to school", "to a poor man with a dog", money and a crane taken by his gerfalcon Corbet given to a poor woman at Down Amney, and a pardon for outlawry granted at the petition of "a poor maimed man who followed him at Down Amney". Other benefits than money he also extended to his subjects, exercising the divine, miraculous gift of healing traditionally inherent in English sovereigns from the days of the Confessor; he is constantly found touching persons afflicted with that particular form of scrofula known as "the king's evil", as many as 288 persons being touched, and given a penny each, in one week in 1278. It was also his endeavour to heal the sores of the body politic by new legislation and, what was really more important, by enquiring into the administration of the existing law. It was from the maladministration, peculation and corruption of the officials, from the Chief Justices of the Bench down to the catchpolls of the manor courts, that the people suffered rather than from the weakness or badness of the laws. To remedy this was Edward's constant endeavour and if he failed it must be remembered that the cleansing of such an Augean stable demanded the efforts of a single-minded Hercules and was bound to be beyond the powers of a king constantly engaged in wars and political struggles with cunning adversaries.

Edward's policy of establishing his own supremacy and freeing the crown from the control of the nobles drove him to seek the support of the people and on at least two occasions we find him making a public speech, not to his parliament, council or courtiers, but to a casual assembly of his subjects. The first and more important occasion was outside Westminster Hall when he was reconciled to Archbishop Winchelsey, with rather theatrical publicity, in 1297; the other was in 1299 before undertaking his Scottish expedition, when he visited the Abbey of St. Albans and, after long prayer, addressed the assembled congregation. On both occasions he emphasized the fact that the wars were undertaken for the preservation of England, pointed out that he was about to risk his own life and made a direct appeal for the prayers and sympathy of his subjects. More important than these direct appeals was the recognition, incomplete but significant, of the principle of no taxation without representation, the control of parliament over the granting of supplies and the extension of representation, culminating in the "Model Parliament" of 1295. In addition to this building up of a popular part Edward took more definite measures against the baronage. The Inquest of *quo warranto*, if it did not greatly curtail the powers already possessed by the great lords, at least restricted further usurpations and emphasised the supremacy of the king as the fount of honour, while the Statute of *Quia Emptores* brought the smaller military tenants and landowners into more direct touch with the crown. More significant still was his skilful manipulation of the great earldoms. Lancaster, Leicester and Derby were held by his brother Edmund, and to these Lincoln and Salisbury were joined by the marriage of Edmund's son Thomas with the daughter and heir of Henry de Lacy. The great earldom of Cornwall, held by his cousin, fell to Edward on the earl's death without heirs and was retained as an appendage of the crown. The dangerously independent earls of Gloucester and Hereford, with their great March estates, were married to royal princesses, and the young holder of the double earldom of Surrey and Sussex, after the death of his grandfather, the loyal old John de Warenne, was similarly honoured with the hand of one of the king's granddaughters. Finally the obstinate Earl Marshal, Bigod of Norfolk, a man of no ability but born great and with greatness thrust upon him by the comparative insignificance of his associates, was persuaded or bullied into surrendering his earldom and marshalship to Edward, by whom they were conferred upon his infant son Thomas of Brotherton. The palatinate earldom of Chester having been in his own hands prior to his accession, Edward by the end of his reign had practically absorbed the whole of the great territorial lordships and brought them within the narrow bounds of the royal family. Had his son and successor resembled him in character and ability a despotic autocracy might have been established which would have altered the whole history of English constitutional history, and it is questionable whether we owe a greater debt to the strength of Edward I, which curbed the baronial oligarchy, or to the weakness of Edward II, which shook the power of the throne and saved England from a despotism.

*Chapter Ten*

# Appendix

### Legal, Constitutional and Financial Background

Law, considered historically, may be divided into two branches, Theory or Legislation, and Practice or Administration. The divergence between these two branches will be found to vary according to the efficiency of the executive, or police force, and the distance of the districts under consideration from the centre of government—that distance being measured not by mileage but by accessibility, for Bombay in the twentieth century is nearer to Westminster than Bungay was in the thirteenth, and communication is easier now between Scotland Yard and New York than it then was between York and the Scottish Border. Edward on his accession to the English throne found the nation in possession of a fairly well developed system of law, simple in outline but complicated on the practical or administrative side by the intrusion or survival of local custom and the multiplicity of jurisdictions. In theory supreme legal authority rested with the King's Court, and ultimately with the king himself. In fact there were below the King's Court other jurisdictions almost innumerable, the sessions of Justices in Eyre, who went on circuit at irregular intervals, the courts of the sheriffs, coroners, escheators and royal bailiffs, courts of counties, hundreds, boroughs, baronies, manors and liberties and the Courts Christian or ecclesiastical courts; and inevitably their jurisdictions overlapped. It was, therefore, part of Edward's task to produce some kind of uniformity in theoretical law, by codification, and in administrative law by defining the rights and duties of the subordinate courts, whether they were those of his own officials or of his feudal tenants. The theoretical supremacy of the king in legal matters was so far practical that his prolonged absence, in Gascony, Wales or Scotland, usually coincided with the periods of greatest lawlessness. In the case of the interval between his accession and his return to England this was aggravated by the extreme feebleness which had characterised the administration of Henry III during his last years. One of his first actions, therefore, after his coronation was to order a general enquiry throughout the kingdom into the universal complaints which had reached his ears, and particularly those relating to the usurpation of crown privileges or estates and to the abuse of their powers by officials.

The result of this general enquiry was embodied in the Hundred Rolls and revealed a state of maladministration and oppression which can only be called appalling. As might be expected, the worst offences were found in the classes of officials furthest removed from the direct supervision of the crown. Against the sheriffs, coroners and escheators as a rule the complaints did not extend beyond venality and extortion, but these offences were practically universal. There was hardly an official who did not, upon occasion if not by custom, take bribes to perform or to neglect his duty. Nor was this surprising in view of the venality of their superiors, the practically open acceptance of bribes by royal justices, which was revealed and punished in 1289 when Edward, like the king in the parable who had gone into a far country, returned and called his unjust ministers to account. Among the deputy sheriffs, bailiffs and, above all, the stewards and other officers of feudal courts, extortion was still more rampant and was accompanied by violence and brutality. The power of imprisoning on simple suspicion or accusation was used mercilessly as a means of extorting gifts. The prisons, terrible enough in ordinary circumstances, were rendered more unbearable by the use of torture; prisoners were kept without food, loaded with irons, bound naked to a post, or hung up by the arms until they were willing to pay for their release. In the summary of the Yorkshire returns "many things beyond number and astonishing" were related of the sub-sheriff, "many acts of oppression, extortion, robbery and injury, beyond belief" were set to the charge of the bailiff of the Earl of Lincoln, "devilish and innumerable acts of oppression" were alleged against the steward of Earl Warenne, and the bailiff of Staincliffe, of whom "many most evil reports" were made, insulted the justice holding the enquiry, threatening to drag him out of the court by his heels because he had directed the jurors to tell the truth without fear. It was a period of violence and Edward's endeavours to maintain order met with very partial success. The little war between the Earls of Gloucester and Hereford in 1290 was only the most notorious of a number of such quarrels. The Hundred Rolls show Earl Warenne carrying on an armed dispute in Sussex with his neighbour, Robert Aguillon, and in 1300 Edward had to intervene to prevent war between the Earl of Warwick and Sir Walter de Beauchamp. The Berkeleys prosecuted their claim to the lordship of Redcliffe in Bristol by armed attacks upon the mayor and his supporters; there were "Town and Gown" riots at Oxford in 1282 and at Cambridge in 1290, while a faction fight between the northern and southern scholars at Oxford in 1296 was used by the townsmen as an excuse for plundering the scholastic hostels. The battle at Swine in 1297 was only the most outstanding incident of the great "Herring War" carried on during the whole of this reign between the sailors of the Cinque Ports and of Yarmouth. There were even numerous cases of the possession of churches being disputed by armed force, the sacred buildings being treated as fortresses and filled with armed men.

Some idea of the reign of violence and the inefficiency of police measures may be gathered from the prevalence of murder at this time. When troops were being raised from the ranks of the criminals for the Scottish war the pardons issued for specified offences were entered on the Patent Rolls. In one single list, dated 10 November 1303, no fewer than 450 persons were pardoned for murders and a further 150 were enrolled between June and August 1304. The evidence of these lists is borne out by the Assize and similar rolls, which show the extraordinary frequency of murder and the comparative rarity of arrests. A few of these murders attracted public attention, as for instance the case of Laurence Duket, a London goldsmith, in 1284. Duket in the course of a quarrel with a clerk, Ralph Crepyn by name, drew his dagger, wounded his adversary and fled into the church of St. Mary le Bowe, probably intending to remain there until he knew whether the blow had been fatal. While he was in sanctuary there Crepyn's mistress, Alice of Gloucester, came and threatened him; next night she returned with several friends and, with the connivance of the clerk of the church, they hanged Duket from a beam, Alice putting the finishing touch to her vengeance by stabbing him to the heart. The case, involving as it did sacrilege, aroused a sensation, the criminals were arrested and condemned, Alice of Gloucester being burnt alive and the others hanged. Eight years later, in 1292, while parliament was sitting at Westminster, Roger de Drayton, the Earl of Cornwall's treasurer, and Richard, constable of Berkhamsted, were attacked in broad daylight in the streets of London and slain by Richard Walrand and his brothers, whose mother the treasurer had maliciously put in the pillory at Berkhamsted. The sympathies of the citizens were so strongly on the side of the Walrands that no attempt was made to arrest them, they were allowed to escape into St. Paul's and, having abjured the realm, were escorted to Dover. In the following year, 1293, the Dunstable annalist briefly records that the Justices in Eyre in Yorkshire acted with great severity towards Sir Simon le Constable. The facts as related in the rolls of the court would seem, to modern ideas, to justify a certain amount of severity. Sir Simon, the head of a wealthy and ancient family, had abducted Katherine, wife of Sir John de Danthorpe, and after the death of Sir John had poisoned his own wife in order to marry Katherine; the facts of the murder, which had been committed in 1283, seem to have been notorious but no action had been taken against Sir Simon, who was constantly employed in a magisterial capacity during the next ten years. At last, in 1293, he was brought before the itinerant justices and charged with the crime; seeing that conviction was certain he sacrificed himself for the good of his heir and saved his estates from forfeiture by refusing to plead. By criminal law no one could be tried by a jury without their own consent; a criminal therefore who refused to plead could not be found guilty of felony,* which would involve the forfeiture of his estates, but compulsion, amounting to a form of torture, could be put upon him to compel him to plead, and accordingly, in this case "the penalty of the statute"—*peine forte et dure*—was inflicted and under it the noble murderer died. What that penalty was is fully described in the case of the bailiff of a Norfolk hundred who refused, in this same year 1293, to plead on an accusation of having murdered certain Dutch sailors—he was to be imprisoned and "on the day on which he eats he shall not drink and the bread which he has shall be of the worst quality and the water which he drinks shall be stagnant and he shall sit naked, save for a linen garment, upon the bare earth and shall be loaded with irons† from the hands to the elbows and from the feet to the knees, until he will submit himself to a jury."

*A curious instance occurs in 1299 of a man being pardoned for a murder on the ground that as he was a deaf mute he could not be tried by jury.

†The weighting with irons eventually developed into the custom of "pressing to death" which continued into the eighteenth century.

It is possible that the severity of the penal code was largely responsible for the apparent reluctance of juries to convict. However that may be, it is certain that convictions were rare and an enormous proportion of prisoners were acquitted in the face of what was either very strong evidence or very circumstantial lying. If one adds to the numbers of prisoners wrongfully acquitted the large number who either evaded arrest altogether or took sanctuary in a church and those who abjured the realm, saving their lives at the expense of banishment, it is evident that very many crimes must have been left unavenged. One of the causes contributing to this was the complication of the police system by the existence of numerous liberties and franchises into which the ordinary officers of the law were not allowed to enter. Out of numerous complaints on this subject we may cite one in 1275 when a gang of robbers in Essex was broken up, some being captured and the others establishing themselves with impunity in the liberties of the Bishop of Ely and the Abbot of St. Edmunds. Next year a commission was appointed to settle the bounds of certain land on the borders of Lincolnshire, Rutland and Leicestershire as owing to its not being assigned to any particular county murders and other crimes were frequent there and went unpunished. Another way in which justice was hindered was by the interference of the Church on behalf of all accused clerks. The number of clerical offenders was very great, though it had not yet reached the dimensions attained in the fifteenth century, and over these the lay courts had no effective jurisdiction, the utmost that they could do being to state whether the accused was guilty or not when they handed him over to the spiritual authority. In the great sack and burning of Boston Fair in 1288, one of the most sensational crimes of the period, a large proportion of the associates* of Robert Chamberlain,

*Sir James Ramsay (p. 365) states that "Thomas (*sic*) Chamberlain was identified and hung, but he refused to disclose the names of any of his accomplices." A large number of names of those involved may, however, be found in Assize Roll 1286.

or Chambers (*de Camera*), were clerks, one of the chief being a monk of Kirkstead, and a church was used as their place of assembly and for hiding the plunder. Amongst those claimed by the Ordinary as clerks on this occasion it is interesting to find a knight, Ranulf de Freskenay, *miles*; and it is also typical of what was said above as to the acquittal of prisoners in spite of evidence, that a clerk, Patrick de Castelcayrok, who is named by every jury as a ringleader, second only to Robert Chamberlain, was found not guilty. The other famous crime, the robbery of the Treasury, was mainly the work of monks, and clerks are to be found involved in every species of offence from poaching to poisoning, while such evidence as we have of the working of the ecclesiastical courts shows that they were as partial and venal as the lay courts, modelling themselves on the papal court of Rome, where venality had been brought to a fine art and Brother *Dabitur* could only be seen on an introduction from Brother *Date*.

The immediate result of the compilation of the Hundred Rolls was the issue at Edward's first parliament, in the spring of 1275, of the First Statute of Westminster. This was a codification, in fifty sections, of the existing laws, with certain modifications, and was remarkably comprehensive. Extortion by royal officers, lawyers, purveyors, clerks of markets, bailiffs and so forth; writs and methods of procedure in criminal and civil processes; admission to bail and seizure of distresses; the privileges of feudal lords with respect to their wards and the exaction of aids from their tenants; the custom of wreck; freedom of elections; the delivery of clerical offenders to their Ordinary; and the limiting of the exaction of hospitality from religious houses; all these subjects are dealt with briefly and clearly. Certain points were subsequently elucidated by a statute defining the duties and qualifications of coroners, another, "*de Bigamis*", of which the most important clause laid down the rule that all clerks twice married were deprived of the benefit of their clergy; and a third, the Statute called Rageman passed in 1276, by which Justices in Eyre were appointed to enquire into all offences and trespasses by officials and others during the past twenty-five years. Another code of importance is contained in the Statute of Wales, issued in 1284. Although this was drawn up for the special purpose of regulating legal procedure in the newly formed shires of the conquered principality it is in effect a complete codification of county court procedure.

The next year, 1285, saw the issue of another code, the Second Statute of Westminster. This, like its predecessor, covered a wide ground and was divided into fifty sections, but from the point of view of the legal historian it is even more important. Without a detailed discussion and comparison, which would be outside the scope of this book, it may be said that the main difference between the two Statutes of Westminster was that the first was a code of general law and the second of special law. The first had been called into existence by the general decay and abuse of the existing law, of which it reaffirmed the principles with only slight amplification. But Law was still in its empiric stage; actual practice raised many problems and revealed many imperfections, and it was to remedy these that the second was designed. Accordingly in this Second Statute of Westminster we find restatements of passages from earlier statutes with explanations or expansions and details of procedure in connection with the more obscure and ingenious infractions of the law. The fraudulent use of the privileges of the Templars and Hospitallers, the responsibility for the debts of intestates, waste committed by one of the joint tenants, the punishment for abducting a nun, are among the subjects treated. Most importance, however, attaches to the first clause, *de donis conditionalibus*, by which, in the case of lands granted on certain conditions (e.g. with reversion in the event of the failure of specified heirs), evasions of the grantor's intentions were checked, and to the rearrangement of the system of justices of assize by the appointment of special justices of *nisi prius* to hold assizes of mortdauncestor and novel disseisin and similar suits, in conjunction with knights of the shire, three times in the year. This statute, therefore, is important both for its interpretation of existing legislation and for its innovations, both alike showing the development of English law on a deliberate and intelligent system, for which King Edward himself may be allowed some credit even if the major part must be assigned to his Chancellor, Robert Burnel, and his associates such as Ralph de Hengham, the venal but learned Chief Justice.

With the greater codifying statutes might be classed the *Articuli super Cartas* of 1300, a series of twenty enactments accepted and promulgated by the king at the time of his reluctant confirmation of Magna Carta and the Forest Charter. These included provisions for enforcing the observance of the Great Charter, restricting purveyance and other abuses, and defining the jurisdictions of the courts of the Household, Exchequer, and of the Constable of Dover, but were not of any outstanding importance. On the administrative side two codes remain to be noticed. The Statute of Gloucester, passed in 1278 as an outcome of the usurpations of privileges revealed in the Hundred Rolls and as a preliminary to their resumption by the proceedings of *quo warranto*, dealt with the abuses of the feudal courts and strengthened the courts of common law at their expense. The Statute of Winchester, issued in the autumn of 1285, covered fairly completely the regulations for the policing of the country, local and national. It was in no way creative but merely re-enacted existing regulations, in some cases of traditional antiquity. In the matter of local police measures we find restated the systems of watch, and hue and cry, and the joint responsibility of the hundred for the detection and repression of crimes; while in the matter of national police we have the Assize of Arms, altered in detail but not in principle since the time of Henry II, by which every man between the ages of fifteen and sixty was bound to keep ready certain weapons, assessed according to his wealth. Contemporary with this Statute of Westminster were certain statutes issued for the City of London for the control of taverns, the suppression of fencing schools, where "fools who delight in mischief" were encouraged in their folly, and the general policing of the streets.

In addition to the codification, expansion and development of law under Edward I there was an important amount of actual innovation, concerned with the three classes of merchants, feudal tenants and clergy. By the Statute of Acton Burnel, issued in 1283, the recovery of trading debts was much expedited and simplified, to the great encouragement of merchants, foreign and English, and presumably to the benefit of trade, though nothing approaching trading statistics can be compiled. In 1290 an important change was introduced into tenurial land law by the Statute of *Quia Emptores*, by which the practice of subinfeudation was checked. By this statute when lands held in fee of a particular lord were sold by the freeholder they were to continue to be held in fee of the original chief lord of the fee and not be held in fee of the freeholder who had sold them. This statute is therefore often said to have put a stop to the formation of new manors, and in theory it did so although there is evidence that new manors did arise after this date, but as a whole subinfeudation was pretty effectually stopped. Much less effective in practice was the check on the alienation of property to religious bodies given by the Statute *de Viris Religiosis* of 1279. Under this statute, better known as the first Mortmain Act, lands granted in future to religious corporations, who were incapable of rendering the military and other services due from them, were *ipso facto* forfeited to the immediate lord of the fee, or, if he neglected to enforce the penalty, to the superior lords in succession and ultimately to the king. The need for such legislation had long been recognised and had formed one of the demands put forward in the Provisions of Oxford in 1258 but it had remained for Edward to give it statutory form. Unfortunately the readiness with which Edward himself and his successors granted licences for the evasion of its provisions rendered it practically a dead letter. A further step to remedy the impoverishment of the nation for the benefit of the monastic orders was taken at the Westminster parliament of 1305, when such English religious houses as were subordinate to foreign chapters, especially the abbeys of the Cistercian and Premonstratensian Orders, were forbidden to send money out of the realm to their mother houses.* At the same time the foreign prelates were forbidden to levy any rents, tallages or taxes upon the English houses of their Order. Although this piece of legislation was passed in 1305 it was temporarily suspended and was not published until two years later, at Edward's last parliament, at Carlisle in January 1307, and was therefore known as the Statute of Carlisle.

From a constitutional point of view it is important to notice what parts were played in the legislation of this reign by the King himself, his Council and the Parliament. Equal legislative force attached to enactments whether they were merely royal ordinances or published with the authority of a full representative parliament. The Statute of Winchester in 1285 and the Forest Ordinance of 1306 were both issued by the king without reference to any other authority; the Statute of Wales was issued "by advice of our nobles", that relating to the suppression of bad money, in 1299, "with the consent of the prelates, earls and barons" and the *Articuli super Cartas* at the request of the same three classes. The Statute of Rageman

---

* This did not apply to the small houses which were cells directly dependent in all ways upon foreign abbeys, but Edward initiated the policy, followed by his successors, of seizing the revenues of these alien priories when at war with France.

was published by the king and his council and that *de Bigamis* was drawn up by a committee of clergy and published "in the presence of the king and his council." In the case of the Statute of Gloucester the king is said to have called together "the more discreet persons of his kingdom, as well of the greater as of the less", and these are elsewhere summed up as his prelates, earls, barons and Council. The Statute of Acton Burnel was passed in 1283 and confirmed, with additions, in 1285 "by the king and council in parliament" and the most complete form is found in the preamble to the First Statute of Westminster, which is said to have been enacted by the king at his parliament by his Council and by the assent of the prelates, earls, barons and commonalty of the realm; while, finally, the Statute of Carlisle is assigned to the advice of the earls, barons, magnates, nobles and commonalty of the realm. It is inadvisable to build much upon the actual wording of records at this period when legal terminology had not become so rigidly defined as it did later and technical terms were used loosely. The line between a council and a parliament was far from well defined and the same assembly might be called by either name. Council in itself was a term of vague significance, being applied alike to the Privy Council, a permanent body composed of sworn members who held the position either in right of their rank as prelates or magnates or by virtue of special summons, the Great Council, consisting of the prelates, higher clergy and that vague body the baronage, or the Common Council, similarly constituted but with the addition of representatives of the commonalty. Parliament, again, was used for sessions of any of these three Councils and it was only after the Common Council had become properly representative of the three estates that the term gradually became narrowed down to imply the national representative assembly.

The separation and development of the three estates of Clergy, Barons and Commons, a gradual and instinctive

o

rather than a deliberate process, is one of the features of Edward's reign. That the division should have been into these three classes was not inevitable. Considered socially the people might be better divided into gentry, including all military tenants from the earl to the knight, peasantry free and unfree, yeoman and villein, and the professional class, merchants, traders and skilled craftsmen. Of these three classes the clergy formed a subdivision, the prelates and higher clergy ranking for all social purposes with the gentry, and the ill-paid, ill-educated parochial clergy and chaplains with the peasantry, while the professional class were represented by the members of the religious orders. A fourth class, socially, which at one time seemed not unlikely to form a fourth estate politically, was formed of the lawyers. Politically, however, the clergy were separated by their privileges and their possessions of a distinct legal system and it was therefore natural that they should constitute a separate caste. The lines of cleavage in the ranks of the laity were not so obvious. Between the earls and the knights and lesser freeholders lay the class distinguished by the title of barons. The exact origin and meaning of the title have led to much discussion, but it is sufficient for our purpose to note that while at the beginning of Edward's reign the title was tenurial, implying the holding of an estate "by barony," that is to say with the obligation of paying certain feudal dues on a special scale,* by the end of his reign baronies were created by, and inherent in, the reception of a special writ of summons to parliament. For some time it was uncertain whether the baronage would join with the earls or would unite with the lower freeholders and leave the earls to form the second estate (the clergy being the first); the creation of baronies by writ marks the definite separation between the barons and the knights and their assimilation

*Where the knight paid a shilling the baron paid a mark (13s. 4d.) and the earl a pound.

to the earls to form the second estate, or House of Lords. The third estate, or commons, differed from the second from a parliamentary point of view in being representative. Whereas all members of the baronage had a theoretical right to attend parliament it was clearly impossible for all members of the commonalty to do so and the first step for their representation was taken by ordering two knights of the shire to be elected by each county;—that is to say by each county court, the attendants at which were the whole body of the freeholders in the county, from the magnates downwards, and the reeve and four men from each township. Exactly who constituted the electors and by what method the elections were conducted is not certain, and indeed it is probable that the customs varied considerably in the different counties; but the knights would seem to have been accepted as reasonably representative and their wages were paid by a levy on the county, which we may assume would not have been the case, or at least would not have passed without protest, if the elective power had not been general. The guiding principle of representation, "that that which touches all shall be approved by all", was definitely put forward by King Edward in his writs of summons for the Model Parliament of 1295 in which that principle was put into practice. As late as 1294, when the knights of the shire had consented to a subsidy of a tenth being levied from the counties, special negotiations had had to be made with the towns for a subsidy of a sixth, but now the parliament was made complete by the return of two representatives from each city and borough. The third estate had thus attained its political fulfilment and from this time parliament was the representative assembly of the three estates.

Finance had been the compelling cause which shaped the growth of parliament and it remained for some time the most important feature of its work. The necessity for parliamentary assent to legislation had not yet been accepted but its necessity in the case of taxation was fully recognised by Edward. On the financial history of the reign, a highly complicated and rather repellent subject, any elaborate disquisition would fortunately be out of place in these pages. It has been dealt with in considerable detail and with an expenditure of much labour by Sir James Ramsay, to whose work readers may be referred. From our point of view, concerned as we are with the personality of Edward, the interest lies rather in the illegal devices to which he resorted upon occasion for the raising of money than in the record of more regular levies. At the same time a few points in regard to the ordinary subsidies, of a tenth, a fifteenth or whatever the proportion may be, are worth brief consideration. The first of these is the method of assessment. In theory the commissioners for every county appointed a committee of twelve who, in turn, were responsible for seeing that the reeve and four men in every township visited every house and made a valuation of all the goods. Taking as an instance the subsidy of the year 1296, when the counties granted a twelfth and the boroughs an eighth, we find first of all that persons having goods worth less than 12d. in the country or 8s. in the towns were exempt from payment; it was also laid down that the armour and harness, jewels and robes of knights and gentlemen and of their wives and their vessels of gold, silver and bronze were not to be valued; similar exemption in the towns was extended to one robe for the man and one for his wife, a bed for the two, one ring, one brooch, of gold or silver, one girdle of silk used every day and a silver cup or mazer from which they drank. The details of the assessment made at this time in Colchester, in which the nets of the fishermen, the coals of the blacksmith, and so forth, are entered, show that in some cases in the towns this inquisitorial procedure was duly followed, and it is not surprising that Edward ordered the business to be entrusted to "persons who know how to speak pleasantly to the people and understand how to conduct the matter well and wisely". In the case of the country districts, it seems clear that the assessment was often made by hundreds and not by townships and while in some hundreds the prevalence of halfpence and farthings points to a conscientiously accurate assessment, in others the absence of these fractions and the large proportion of round figures indicates that the assessors were content to levy a sum approximately corresponding to the known wealth or poverty of the assessed. As regards the amount produced by these levies, it would seem that the average yield of a fifteenth was between £80,000 and £100,000 and that therefore subsidies may be roughly estimated on the basis of a national wealth in movables of £1,500,000, equivalent to something like thirty millions in modern money. In the matter of clerical subsidies we have the advantage of the careful valuation produced by order of Pope Nicholas IV in 1291, which shows that the clergy paid on a basis of about £210,000; the tenth, therefore, which was the most usual proportion granted, was roughly £20,000, and the half extorted in 1294 would have yielded £100,000 if it had been paid in full, as it almost certainly was not. Besides the grants which the clergy made of their own free will, or at least through the medium of their Convocation, there were crusading tenths levied for six years from 1291 by papal authority, of which the king seems to have received three-quarters, the remaining quarter being reserved to the Pope.

Not only did Edward appropriate to his own uses this money intended for crusading purposes but in 1283, acting with the same impetuosity which had led him in his younger days to seize the treasure in the Temple, he laid hands on the money collected for a crusade, of which the Pope had definitely refused to grant him any portion. In this case he realised his mistake, returned the money and was able to assume an air of injured innocence when Archbishop Pecham presented him with the Pope's indignant demand for its restoration. Twenty years later he again acted with more ingenuity than honesty. It would seem that in 1301 Pope Boniface VIII granted King Edward the half of a clerical tenth for three years; on the death of Boniface at the end of 1303 Edward claimed that by the terms of the grant the whole tenth now belonged to him and he at once issued orders for its collection. A protest being made on behalf of the new Pope Benedict XI, the king wrote* to Treasurer Langton that it had never been the custom to recognise a pope until he had sent an official notification of his election and of the name which he had assumed. As soon as this had been done the customary royal present of jewels (*beaux joyeaux*) would be despatched, and then messengers should be sent to him to discuss the question of the second half of the tenth; meanwhile the whole was to be levied to the king's use.

Any reliable estimate of the king's total revenue is remarkably difficult to obtain. Sir James Ramsay estimates that whereas the average revenue of Henry III was about £40,000, occasionally rising to £50,000, that of his son was approximately double, varying from £80,000 to £100,000, and this is probably as near as it is possible to get without an excessive expenditure of minute research. The issues of the Crown estates, including Ireland, whose only appearance in the records of this reign is as a source of income, the sheriffs' ferms, or rents of counties, and the customs formed the bulk of the permanent revenue, varying only slightly from year to year. There were also every year what we may call judicial issues, fines levied in the various courts for infractions of the law and other fines paid for the renewal of charters or other acts of royal grace. Issues of mines also must not be ignored, the lead and silver mines of Cumberland, the Peak and Devonshire bringing in large sums, while the "coinage" duties on tin during the

* Anct. Correspondence (P.R.O.) xii, 184, xiii, 114.

last seven years of Edward's reign when the Cornish mines were in his hands by the death of the Earl of Cornwall were well over £1,000. Edward seems to have taken great interest in the mining industry, as it was particularly active during his reign and he is several times found bringing over experts from Germany to work the royal mines, more particularly in Ireland, where gold was certainly discovered, as in 1287 he had in his Wardrobe a bar of Irish gold, of which he gave half to Queen Eleanor. The Devonshire mines served also as pledges on the security of which he raised money from Italian merchants on some of the numerous occasions when his expenses were in excess of his revenue. The part played at this time in international finance, and therefore in international history, by the Italian merchants was very important but cannot be dealt with here. Nor is it profitable or possible here to follow in detail the constant struggles to meet the heavy expenditure involved by wars with France and Wales and Scotland, the expedients tried and their varying measures of success. So far as they are concerned with Edward's personality they have already been mentioned and it is in their personal and political aspects that their importance for us lies. Whatever errors or injustices there were in Edward's financial operations, however much his people groaned under taxation, it may be asserted in his justification that the money was levied for no selfish or mean purposes but for what he honestly believed to be the true good of the nation.

# Sources

Here are listed the principal sources on which this study is based.
Manuscripts at the Public Record Office: Exchequer K.R. Accounts
—particularly the Wardrobe and Household Accounts. Ancient
Correspondence, and Ancient Petitions. Pipe Rolls; Liberate
Rolls; Memoranda Rolls. *Printed Calendars* of Patent, Close, and
Charter Rolls; Miscellaneous Inquisitions; Papal Registers.
The *Hundred*, and *Quo Warranto* Rolls. *Feudal Aids; Book
of Fees. Rolls of Parliament*; and Palgrave's *Parliamentary Writs.*
Rymer's *Foedera*; Wilkins, *Concilia*; Stubbs, *Select Charters.*
*Political Songs* (ed. T. Wright for Camden Society). Bain, *Cal.
of Documents relating to Scotland. The Exchequer Rolls of Scotland*,
vol. 1.

Chronicles: The Rolls Series: particularly Matthew Paris, *Historia*
and continuation as *Flores Historiarum*; John of Oxnead;
Bartholomew Cotton; Walter Hemingburgh; Nicholas Trivet;
Robert of Gloucester; Pierre de Langtoft; *Annales Monastici*;
*Brut-y-Tywysogion*; Register of Archbishop Peckham. Gale,
*Scriptores Rerum Anglorum.* Wharton, *Anglia Sacra: Liber de
Antiquis Legibus* (ed. Riley).

Itineraries: Itineraries for many individual years will be found
among Joseph Hunter's notes in the British Museum (Add.
Chs.25409–25412). *Itineraries* for the whole reign were published
by C. H. Hartshorn in 1871 and by H. Gough in 1900. The
Itinerary of Edward into Scotland was printed in *Archaeologia*
vol. XXI; and that into France in 1286–1289 was the subject
of a particularly valuable article by J. P. Trebut-Cussac in the
*Bulletin of the Institute of Historical Research* for 1952.

# Bibliography

The amount of matter printed in books and articles concerning
various aspects of the reign is formidable; the Bibliography in
Powicke's *Thirteenth Century* runs to 50 pages. Attention may be
called to the following: Stubbs, *Constitutional History*; Maitland,
*Constitutional History*; Pollock and Maitland, *History of English Law*;
Sir J. H. Ramsay, *Dawn of the Constitution*; Sir Maurice Powicke,
*Henry III and the Lord Edward*, and *The Thirteenth Century* (Oxford
Hist. of England); F. W. Tout, *Edward I*, and other works; Helen
Cam, *Liberties and Communities in Mediaeval England*; Bouquet,
*Recueil des Historiens de la France*; Champollion-Figueac, *Documents
Inédits.*

# Index